Home Winemaking

with Step-by-step Pictures

Home Winemaking

with Step-by-step Pictures

by Paul and Ann Turner

W. Foulsham & Co. Ltd.
London · New York · Toronto
Cape Town · Sydney

W. Foulsham & Company Limited,
Yeovil Road, Slough, Berkshire SL1 4JH

ISBN 0-572-01173-3

Designed by Stonecastle Graphics

Photoset by Rowland Phototypesetting Ltd
Bury St Edmunds, Suffolk

Printed in Hong Kong

Contents

Introduction 7

Equipment 9

Fermentation 13

The hydrometer 20

Your first wine 25

Racking and clearing your wine 35

Bottling, corking, and labelling 43

Storing and blending your wines 50

Wines from concentrates and canned fruit 53

Sparkling wine 60

Mead 66

Weights, measures, & their abbreviations 70

Picking Wild Plants 70

Poison—not to be taken 71

Spring recipes 73

Summer recipes 83

Autumn recipes 92

Winter recipes 102

Serving wine 112

What went wrong? 114

Glossary 115

Index 118

Further reading 120

Introduction

Home winemaking has rapidly become a popular pastime. Rightly so, because it is a pleasant, fascinating way to produce delicious alcoholic drink easily and cheaply at home.

This highly illustrated book has been designed for the beginner who, having decided to 'take the plunge', requires a basic guide to the seemingly difficult techniques of winemaking. The key word to this book is simplicity, both in text and layout, and if the straightforward step-by-step directions are followed, successful winemaking should be easy. The beginner can start with utensils that are readily available in the kitchen, together with one or two extra, but essential, pieces of equipment, such as a fermentation jar and *fermentation or air lock*.

Fermentation is the most important process in winemaking, and it is probably the most fascinating for the winemaker. *Yeast* is a 'plant' which grows in the presence of sugar, converting it into alcohol and carbon dioxide. Vigorous bubbling is the sign that fermentation has started, and the colourless carbon dioxide gas can be seen escaping as bubbles through a water-filled fermentation lock. One of the pleasures of winemaking is to watch the daily progress of a gallon of the fermenting liquor, until the rhythmic air lock bubbling slows and eventually ceases when fermentation is complete. This process, together with every stage of winemaking, from preparing ingredients to storing and serving wine is fully explained, and illustrated with drawings, step-by-step photographs, and diagrams to show exactly what happens.

There are, of course, many recipes using the cornucopia of fruit, vegetables, flowers, and foliage for home winemaking. It is not surprising, therefore, that a major part of this book is allocated to some of them. The recipes are arranged in seasons so that wine can be made throughout the year.

As interest and experience develop, the wealth of hints, ideas, and practical advice in this book will prove to be of great assistance in this most pleasant of hobbies.

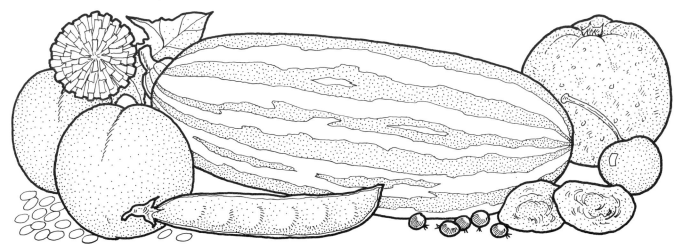

Equipment

There is no need for the beginner to buy lots of expensive equipment straight away but one or two inexpensive items will be needed. As enthusiasm and experience develop, extra equipment will undoubtedly be required. Any equipment that you do need to buy can be obtained from most chemists' shops, many chain stores, some health-food shops, and, particularly, from one of the specialist home brewing and winemaking retailers that can now be found in most towns around Britain.

If there is a 'golden rule' for winemaking, it must be to ensure that all utensils are always clean and free from bacteria. To achieve perfect cleanliness you must wash out, or soak, all your winemaking equipment in a sulphite solution before you use it. You can make a sulphite solution by dissolving either two *Campden tablets* or 1 teaspoonful of *sodium metabisulphite* powder in 1 pint (0·56 litres) of water. The solution is an effective killer of the vinegar-producing bacteria carried by the ever-present fruit fly (*Drosophila melanogaster*) which is probably the winemaker's most persistent enemy.

You should try to obtain all of the following utensils which are essential for successful winemaking.

Boiling pan

You will certainly need some sort of pan for boiling water. It should be large enough to hold at least a gallon (4·5 litres) of liquid, although you will find that a larger vessel is more convenient to work with. A large preserving pan or saucepan may be used, but whatever its size, it is most important that the container should be made of stainless steel, aluminium, or enamel ware. You should not use equipment made of other metals at any stage of your winemaking because they may impart unpleasant flavours to the wine or even deposit poisonous substances.

Fermentation vessel

High-density polythene or polypropylene buckets are ideal for mashing ingredients and initial fermentation purposes, although they should be white or translucent because some buckets or dustbins are not suitable for holding food. Specially designed fermentation bins are widely available. These are usually supplied with a tightly fitting lid which often has a hole for a fermentation lock, to avoid contamination from airborne bacteria. These usually come in two sizes, 5 gallon (25 litre) and 2 gallon (10 litre) and which one you choose will depend on how much wine you plan to make in one go. Large earthenware, plastic or glass containers are also suitable, but don't use earthenware unless you are sure that the glaze has no lead in it. As they will be used for mashing and soaking the fruit, flowers, or berries to extract their flavour, it is essential that the containers are covered to keep out bacteria. Polythene sheeting placed over the top of the container and tied tightly is extremely successful. This allows gas to escape while protecting the liquid from contamination.

Opposite: A selection of useful wine making equipment which can be gathered as experience develops.

9

Fermentation jar

A couple of 1 gallon (5 litre), glass fermentation jars are essential and these are available in both clear and coloured glass. The coloured glass jars are used mainly to avoid the loss of colour from red wine, which sometimes occurs if it is left in daylight for too long. Both types of jar have a narrow neck into which a cork or rubber *bung* can be fitted securely.

Fermentation lock

There is a variety of locks to choose from, made either from glass or plastic. The plastic ones, of course, are less likely to be broken.

The fermentation lock is a simple device which allows gas to escape from the fermenting wine while preventing air or fruit flies from entering the fermentation jar.

Half fill the lock with water, containing a small amount of sulphite solution or an eighth of a Campden tablet. This ensures that, even if fruit flies get into the water in the fermentation lock, it will not become infected, and the risk of any harmful bacteria reaching the fermenting wine is reduced. A small plug of cotton wool placed in the open end of the lock also helps to keep out fruit flies.

The fermentation lock is held firmly in the neck of the fermentation jar by a large rubber bung or cork with a hole in the centre. If you use a cork, you must make sure that it does not dry out and shrink or the air-tight seal will be broken.

Miscellaneous

A large polythene funnel—at least 6 inches (15 centimetres) in diameter—is extremely useful, and no doubt will be found in the kitchen, as will wooden or polypropylene spoons, scales for weighing ingredients, and a clear plastic or glass measuring jug.

During the course of making wine, you will need to strain the liquid. A nylon sieve is the most convenient utensil for removing the larger particles of unwanted deposits, but for straining off finer particles, you should use a jelly bag or a fine-mesh nylon straining bag.

When fermentation has finished, the wine will stop bubbling and begin to clear as all the sugar will have been converted to alcohol and the *specific gravity* of the wine will be close to 1·000 (*see* the chapter on 'The hydrometer', page 20). This should take two or three weeks. Then you will need to siphon off the clear wine from the deposit of dead yeast cells which have fallen to the bottom of the fermentation jar. You should avoid disturbing the waste material, and you can easily make a simple siphon from a length of plastic tubing specially made for the purpose, although you can also buy a more sophisticated siphon incorporating bellows to start the initial flow of liquid.

A thermometer is a handy instrument to have available, and will take the guesswork out of controlling the correct temperature for adding yeast to the liquid and keeping the fermenting wine at its maximum efficiency. It is best to buy a thermometer that has been specially designed for brewing or winemaking. They are usually about 1 foot (30 centimetres) long to give a clear reading and are filled with alcohol rather than mercury so that the wine will not be ruined if the thermometer is broken. If this should happen, the glass will safely remain in the dead yeast cells and the wine can be siphoned from it. Thermometers may be graduated in either Centigrade or Fahrenheit (or both) and range from $-10°C$ ($14°F$) to $110°C$ ($230°F$).

Many items of equipment will be found in most kitchens.

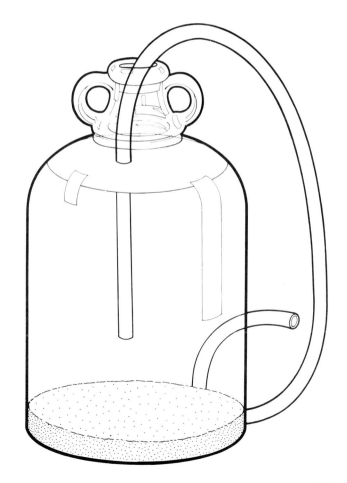

Fermentation

The fact that alcohol is produced by the fermentation of sugar solution by yeast under favourable conditions has been known and utilized for centuries. Winemaking was usually a process of guesswork, which all too often resulted in a product of dubious strength and quality, and frequently in complete failure.

It is only comparatively recently that fermentation has been widely understood, allowing the amateur winemaker a degree of control over the craft that was once impossible to attain.

In home winemaking, fermentation is a complex process in which the microscopic cells of yeast thrive and reproduce themselves on the liquid sugar and fruit juice mixtures, known as *must*. Alcohol is produced by this fermentation and the liquid eventually becomes wine. These living yeast cells have to multiply rapidly to produce the millions needed to convert all the sugar present into alcohol.

As the yeast begins to multiply, it splits the sugar into carbon dioxide and alcohol. A steadily bubbling fermentation will, therefore, be producing alcohol at roughly the same rate as carbon dioxide gas is escaping from the mixture.

It is not at all difficult to make a must ferment and become alcoholic, but several factors determine the quality, strength, and flavour of the finished wine.

Yeast

There are many types of wine yeast available now, some of which will produce a wine with the characteristics of a commercial product such as Bordeaux, Sauternes, port, and burgundy. Obviously, these have to be used in conjunction with ingredients that are sympathetic to their original counterparts.

Wine yeasts are available from your home winemaking stockist in many forms, the most common being dried granules or tablets, although liquid yeasts and cultures are also quite suitable. Some wine yeasts have been developed to allow a greater proportion of alcohol to be produced in the wine than is usually obtainable. You should never be tempted to use brewer's or baker's yeast for winemaking.

A starter bottle

Your must will begin to ferment more quickly and reliably if you start the yeast fermenting in a *starter bottle* before it is added to the must. Prepare a boiled solution of ½ pint (0·5 litre) of fruit juice, 1 ounce (28 grams) of sugar, a pinch of citric acid crystals, and a pinch of winemaker's vitaminized *yeast nutrient*. The addition of the acid and the nutrient should ensure that the conditions are ideal for the yeast to become activated. When the liquid is lukewarm, at about 21°C (70°F), add the sachet of granulated dried yeast or the yeast tablet following the instructions on the packet. Pour the solution into a sterilized bottle, plug the bottle with cotton wool and leave it to stand in a warm place. After a while the liquid will begin to bubble, and it is then ready to be added to the must to produce rapid fermentation.

Opposite: A selection of wine yeasts which are available from home winemaking stockists.

Prepare a solution suitable for a starter bottle.

Pour the mixture into a sterilized bottle.

Add a sachet of dried yeast.

Plug the neck of the bottle with cotton wool.

14

The starter bottle will soon show signs of fermentation.

Yeast nutrient

The addition of a level teaspoonful of yeast nutrient to the must ensures that there is enough nourishment for the yeast in the form of minerals, vitamins, and salts.

Grape juice is the perfect medium for fermentation to take place in, but a proprietary yeast nutrient will provide the correct amount of ammonium sulphate and phosphate in musts lacking these elements.

Vitamin B is also helpful in producing a vigorous fermentation, and is usually found in yeast nutrients, although you can also add vitamin B tablets from time to time to enliven the fermentation.

Temperature

It is most important to maintain the correct temperature in the must because yeast will be killed by too high a temperature and its propagation slowed down or stopped by too low a temperature. The ideal range is between 19°C and 24°C (66–75°F), although a few degrees either way will be tolerated.

Try to make sure that the temperature remains steady by placing the jar out of harm's way in a warm kitchen or airing cupboard.

Acidity

For a vigorous fermentation to take place, the liquid must should be slightly acid. Many fruits contain enough acid naturally, but you will need to add acid to a number of recipes in the form of orange juice, lemon juice, or powdered citric acid. Some authorities also recommend the use of other acids such as tartaric, malic, or lactic acids.

It is often possible to taste the presence of acid in the must but a more reliable method is to test it with the special indicator papers designed for the job and sold in small books or rolls. A leaf of the paper is torn out, dipped into the must and the colour that appears is matched against a colour chart. Acidity can be measured in terms of pH numbers 1 to 14, which actually represent the hydrogen ion concentration, but it is enough to know that low numbers, ie below 7, represent an acid solution whereas high numbers indicate alkali. You should aim for a pH of 3 or 4. More elaborate methods of assessing acidity are available, but unnecessary for the beginner.

Dip a piece of acid indicator paper into the must.

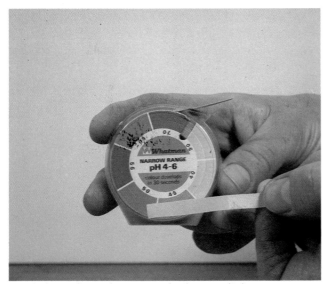

Match the resulting colour against the chart supplied.

A few fruits contain more acid than is normally required, and will impart an unpleasantly sharp taste to the finished wine unless this is corrected during fermentation. Raspberries and rhubarb are in this category, and it is wise to neutralize some of their acidity by adding precipitated chalk in small amounts. Again, you can use the *p*H papers to determine the correct level.

Sugar

Many people believe that the more sugar added to the must, the more alcohol will be produced in the wine. This is only partly true because yeast needs the correct amount of sugar to ensure its maximum efficiency. The optimum quantity of sugar is approximately 2½ pounds of sugar to each gallon of liquid (250 grams per litre). This is the amount which will be used up by the yeast to ferment to its highest possible strength of about 15 per cent alcohol (by volume). When this strength has been reached the yeast will be destroyed by the alcohol it has made, and fermentation will cease.

There are some wine yeasts, however, which have been specially developed to produce a strength of up to 18 per cent alcohol (by volume), but these need not concern the beginner.

If you use too much sugar, it is likely that the fermentation will become sluggish and finish too soon, leaving a large proportion of unfermented sugar in an understrength wine.

Usually, the most successful way of arriving at a wine of the right strength and sweetness is by adding sugar in stages throughout the fermentation.

Add perhaps half the total quantity specified in the recipe at the outset and the remainder in 4 ounce (say, 100 gram) amounts as the fermentation slows. The *hydrometer* is a useful instrument to calculate the final percentage of alcohol (*see* the chapter on 'The hydrometer', page 20).

Ordinary white granulated sugar is the most commonly used and best type to use, although you may like to try the same quantities of brown sugar to produce an attractive flavour in some heavier wines although it will also tend to impart a golden colour. You could certainly use caster sugar or icing sugar but they are more expensive and no better than granulated sugar.

Honey and golden syrup are also suitable for making some wines, but you should only use these as a small proportion of the total sugar content, to avoid 'off' flavours. Honey will give about 75 per cent as much alcohol as sugar.

Most types of sugar and honey can be used to make wine.

Invert sugar (you will need 50 per cent more) may also be used for winemaking. This is sugar which has been chemically split into its two components, glucose and fructose. As the yeast usually has to perform this reaction, invert sugar allows early fermentation to proceed more rapidly, but it is much more expensive and probably unnecessary.

Tannin

Tannin is also required in certain recipes and, in small quantities, it will improve the taste of many wines. It occurs naturally in the skins and stems of fruit, but in wines made from other ingredients it can be added either in the form of strong tea solution, at the rate of one tablespoonful to each gallon of must (approximately 1 millilitre per litre), or as wine tannin sold specifically for the purpose.

Small amounts of tannin will help to clear the must during fermentation and improve the keeping properties of the wine.

The two stages of fermentation

Fermentation of the must, which is the fruit or vegetable extract, sugar, and water to which has been added citric acid, tannin, *pectin*-destroying enzyme, yeast nutrient, and yeast, is usually started in a polythene bucket or fermentation bin. The vessel must be well covered by a lid or sheet of plastic tied tightly to keep fruit flies at bay. This is the first stage, and is called *aerobic* fermentation

Cover the fermentation bin securely with a sheet of plastic.

Transfer the fermenting must to a glass fermentation jar.

As the wine clears, a deposit forms at the bottom of the jar.

because it takes place in contact with air. Aerobic fermentation is vigorous and lasts about four or five days, after which time it settles down. At this stage, the must can be transferred to a sterilized fermentation jar without the risk of the liquid bubbling over. It is advisable, however, to leave some room in the jar for any further activity of the fermenting must. The neck of the jar should be sealed with a fermentation lock to make the container air-tight.

This is the second stage, known as *anaerobic* fermentation, which takes place in the absence of air. After a few weeks of constant activity the mixture becomes progressively less active until, eventually, the yeast has produced all the alcohol it can, and fermentation ceases as the yeast is destroyed.

During this period, which can take four months or more, the must will change from a thick, cloudy 'soup' to a clear liquid with a separate deposit of dead yeast cells and unwanted solids, called the *lees*, which forms at the bottom of the jar. It is a gradual transformation at first, but an improvement in the colour and clarity of the liquid can be seen as the fermentation slows down.

'Sticking' fermentations

Occasionally, a must will start fermenting normally but will cease working after a short period of time. This condition is known as a 'sticking' fermentation and can be caused by one of several factors.

As we have seen already, the correct temperature is most important in maintaining a steady fermentation.

Another cause of a sticking fermentation is the lack of sufficient yeast nutrient or acid in the must. The addition of another teaspoonful of vitaminized yeast nutrient, or a teaspoonful of citric acid will usually get the fermentation under way again.

If you have used an inferior yeast, it is possible that it has reached its alcohol tolerance limit and cannot go on working. To rectify this, prepare a starter bottle from a wine yeast that has been specially developed to go on working in higher concentrations of alcohol and introduce this to the must when it is fermenting vigorously.

You should also make sure that a fermentation which appears to have stuck has not actually used up all the sugar from the must and finished normally.

The hydrometer

Although it is not absolutely essential to use a hydrometer to be able to produce good wine, it is a most useful aid, and will ensure consistent results.

The hydrometer is an instrument which measures the specific gravity (the mass of the liquid compared to that of water which has an S.G. of 1·000) of a liquid. It consists of a long glass or plastic tube weighted at the bottom, and with a scale of figures marked down its length. The smallest figure is at the top and the largest figure at the bottom. This scale enables the winemaker to calculate how much natural sugar is present in the must, and how much will have to be added to achieve a wine of a predetermined alcoholic content.

As more sugar is added to a liquid, it becomes denser (its specific gravity increases), allowing objects to float in it more easily. If you continue to dissolve sugar in a liquid with a hydrometer floating in it, you will see that gradually the hydrometer floats higher and higher as the specific gravity of the liquid increases.

The first calculation to make with the hydrometer is to determine the amount of natural sugar that is present in the must. This will give you the opportunity to adjust the S.G. of your must by either diluting it with water, or adding sugar, to give the potential alcohol content to suit you according to the following table. This is important because some ingredients make a sweeter must than others, and the amount of sugar to be added for a correct fermentation to take place will have to be adjusted accordingly.

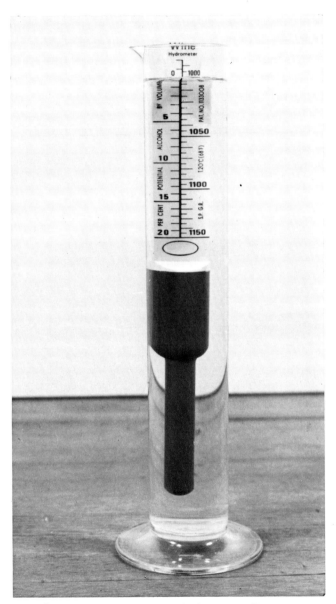

A liquid with little sugar gives a low hydrometer reading.

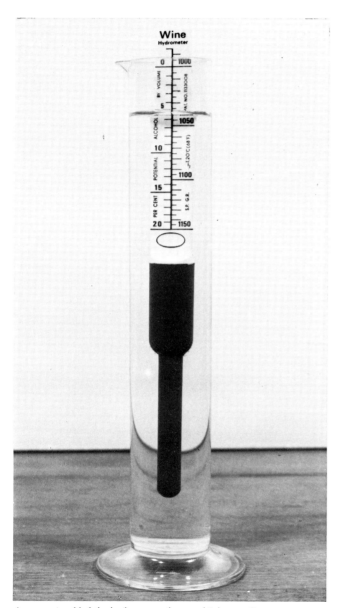

As sugar is added the hydrometer shows a higher reading.

Taking a reading

Pour some of the must into a hydrometer float jar or suitably tall transparent vessel, until it is nearly full. Place the hydrometer in the liquid, heavy end downwards, and rotate it briskly to dislodge air bubbles that may be clinging to it. Usually, the hydrometer should be used in liquids at a temperature of 15·5°C (59·9°F) because most instruments are designed to work accurately at this temperature.

When the hydrometer is floating perfectly still, and not touching the sides of the jar, take a reading. Make sure that your eyes are at the surface level of the must when you look at it. The figure on the graduated scale that is level with the surface of the liquid, ignoring the meniscus, shows the specific gravity.

Pour some must into a hydrometer float jar.

Rotate the hydrometer briskly to remove air bubbles.

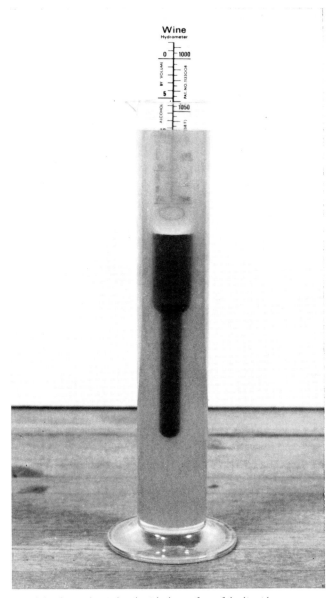

Read the figure that is level with the surface of the liquid.

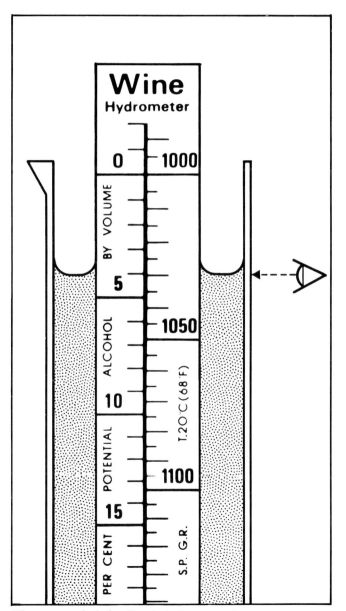

The correct method of reading the hydrometer scale.

By consulting the following table, it is easy to determine how much sugar the must contains.

Specific gravity	Amount of sugar oz./gal.	g./5 l.	Potential alcohol by volume per cent
1010	2	62	0·9
1015	4	123	1·6
1020	7	216	2·3
1025	9	277	3·0
1030	12	370	3·7
1035	15	462	4·4
1040	17	524	5·1
1045	19	585	5·8
1050	21	647	6·5
1055	23	708	7·2
1060	25	770	7·8
1065	27	832	8·6
1070	29	893	9·2
1075	31	955	9·9
1080	33	1016	10·6
1085	36	1109	11·3
1090	38	1170	12·0
1095	40	1232	12·7
1100	42	1294	13·4
1105	44	1355	14·1
1110	46	1417	14·9
1115	48	1478	15·6
1120	50	1540	16·3
1125	52	1602	17·0
1130	54	1663	17·7
1135	56	1725	18·4

You should bear in mind that these figures are not entirely accurate because the solids in the must at the beginning of fermentation and the alcohol at the end do obscure the results, but you can rely on the table as a good working guide.

The table also shows the percentage of alcohol by volume that is likely to be present in the finished wine for different amounts of sugar in the must. Compare the hydrometer reading taken from the must with the specific gravity column of the table. The figure that is closest to your reading will show you the potential alcohol content for that amount of sugar.

To increase the potential percentage of alcohol, simply add more sugar to the must, dissolving it a little at a time, until the hydrometer reading is reached that corresponds to the figure required for your chosen alcoholic strength.

As mentioned earlier, however, yeast will only make about 15 per cent of alcohol by volume. This means that it is pointless to add more sugar than the yeast will be able to use in fermentation, in the hope of achieving a higher alcoholic content. All that will result is a wine that is too sweet to be palatable.

Calculating the final strength

Alcohol has a lower specific gravity than water. During the fermentation, the specific gravity of the must will begin to drop, as sugar is converted into alcohol. If the initial specific gravity is recorded, it is a simple procedure to work out the final strength of the wine.

When the wine has completely finished fermenting, take a hydrometer reading. (At this point you should record a reading of between 1·000 and 1·010.) Omitting the decimal point for this sum, subtract this figure from the initial reading. This will give you the overall drop during fermentation. Divide this number by 7·36 and you will arrive at the percentage of alcohol by volume in the wine.

Example

initial specific gravity	1115
final specific gravity	1003
overall drop	112

$112 \div 7·36 = 15·2$ per cent alcohol by volume

It is possible that your final hydrometer reading is less than 1·000, in which case your wine will be very dry. But don't forget that a really dry wine can always be sweetened to your own taste.

Your first wine

It is nececessary to bear in mind all the points in 'Fermentation' to ensure that you have provided the ideal conditions for a healthy fermentation.

Preparing the must

Wine can be made from a wide variety of ingredients, ranging from wild fruits and berries to flowers, vegetables, and even the left-overs from the teapot. Therefore, there are various ways of preparing a must and you should study carefully the ingredients list and instructions for the correct quantities and method for each wine in the recipe sections.

Before you prepare the must, make sure that all the utensils you intend to use are clean, and that you have sterilized them in a solution of 1 level teaspoon of sodium metabisulphite in 1 pint (0·56 litre) of hot water. You can also add a few crystals of citric acid which help to release sulphur dioxide, the active agent. This should become routine whenever wine-making utensils are used.

Now is the time to extract as much flavour and colour from the ingredients as possible, and this can be done in several ways.

Boiling
Many root vegetables and some fruits are hard, and boiling is the most effective way of extracting the goodness from them. They should be boiled in a stainless steel or aluminium pan, taking care to avoid vigorous boiling. Gentle simmering is best because this is less likely to release any pectin or

Sterilize all utensils in sodium metabisulphite.

Simmer root vegetables in a boiling pan.

Strain the liquid into a fermentation bin.

Strain the liquid again, through a fine-mesh nylon bag.

starch present into the liquid, which would result in a cloudy wine that is stubborn to clear. When the vegetables are soft, the liquid is strained off into a plastic bucket or fermentation bin. You should strain the liquid first through a nylon sieve, and then through a fine-mesh nylon bag to remove the smallest particles.

Soaking in boiling water

This method consists of pouring boiling water on to the ingredients in the fermentation vessel.

The ingredients are then mashed with a wooden spoon, and when cool a pectin-destroying enzyme is added. Yeast may also be added at this stage depending on the recipe.

The fermentation bin is covered with a tightly fitting lid, or plastic sheeting tied securely with string, and left for three or four days, stirring the liquid daily.

Pour boiling water over the ingredients in a fermentation bin.

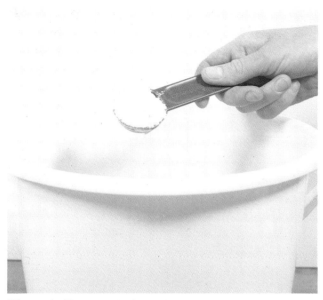

When cool add some pectin-destroying enzyme.

Mash with a wooden spoon.

Cover the fermentation bin securely with a sheet of plastic.

27

Opposite: Soak the ingredients in cold water for several days, stirring the mixture daily to extract the flavour.

Soaking in cold water

This is the most usual way of preparing the must, and it is the simplest. The ingredients are steeped in cold water for several days, stirring daily to extract the flavour.

Yeast may be introduced at the beginning of this period so that fermentation starts immediately, or you can add it after three or four days.

As the fruit contains wild yeasts and bacteria which may prove harmful to the must, it is necessary to destroy them by adding a Campden tablet to the mixture. Just crush a Campden tablet between two spoons, dissolve the powder in a small amount of water, and then add it to the must.

After several days, strain the must and return it to a clean fermentation bin or bucket.

Campden tablets can be crushed between two spoons.

Add a yeast starter bottle.

After several days strain the must into a clean fermentation bin.

Juice extraction

Sometimes the best method of obtaining the most goodness from certain fruits is to use a hand-operated wine press. The obvious candidates for this method are grapes, apples, pears, and other fruits and berries which contain a lot of juice.

First, cut up or mash the fruit and place it in the press, a little at a time. Collect the juice extracted from the fruit in a fermentation jar via a funnel to avoid spilling any.

A modern electric juice extractor, which separates juice from pulp, is an easier way of obtaining fruit juice quickly and efficiently.

Juice extracted by either method can be fermented as it is, straight from the press, or it can be diluted with water to make it more economical and to avoid too strong a flavour. For example, 2 pints (1·2 litres) of pure apple juice together with 1 pound (450 grams) of sugar, and 1 pound (450 grams) of sultanas can be made up with water, pectin-destroying enzyme, yeast, and vitaminized yeast nutrient to make a gallon (4·5 litres) of white table wine. You can start the fermentation immediately and you may also add the pulp to the juice if you want a wine with more body.

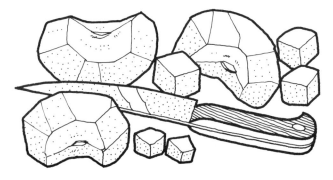

Squeeze the fruit in a wine press to extract the juice.

The juice can be fermented straight from the press.

Adding the yeast

Whichever way you prepare the must, the procedure for adding yeast to the liquid is the same.

The first thing to do is to test the must for acidity with indicator paper and add enough citric acid or lemon juice to bring the acidity to *p*H 3 or 4. If the must is too acid, add precipitated chalk (*see* page 16.) When the acidity is correctly adjusted, take a hydrometer reading and add the necessary amount of sugar (in stages) to arrive at a reading of approximately 1·100 for a dry wine or 1·120 for a sweet wine. It is a good idea to record the reading so that you can determine the final strength of the wine later.

Make sure that the temperature of the must is between 19°C and 24°C (66 to 75°F) before adding your yeast starter (*see* page 13). Don't forget the vitaminized yeast nutrient. Then cover the fermentation bin securely.

Fermentation will begin, quite violently at first, and you should allow it to continue in the fermentation bin for about four or five days. Now transfer the must to a sterilized fermentation jar, leaving enough room for any further vigorous bubbling to take place without overflowing. Fit a fermentation lock partially filled with sulphite solution.

Place the jar in a warm place and then you can watch the progress of the fermentation as carbon dioxide gas escapes in bubbles through the lock.

Test the acidity of the must.

Add a yeast starter bottle and yeast nutrient.

Take a hydrometer reading and add sugar as necessary.

Cover the fermentation bin securely.

The must will soon begin to ferment.

Fit a fermentation lock partially filled with sulphite solution.

Strain the must into a sterilized fermentation jar.

Label the jar and leave to ferment in a warm place.

Racking and clearing your wine

During the first few weeks, or months, of fermentation the must will be a thick, opaque liquid, with a suspension of particles of yeast and pulp, creating an overall *haze*.

As yeast is used up in producing alcohol, the dead cells fall to the bottom of the fermentation jar together with the unwanted particles of fruit or vegetable pulp. The thick deposit or lees must be separated from the clear wine to avoid any unpleasant taste that may develop if it is left in the wine for too long. Therefore, you will need to siphon off or *rack* the clear wine from the lees using your length of clear plastic tubing or specially designed siphon.

Above: After some time the wine will clear, leaving a solid lees.
Opposite: A thick fermenting must bubbling rapidly.

Racking

Stand the fermentation jar of wine to be racked on a table, and place another clean, sterilized jar on the floor beneath it. Remove the fermentation lock and bung, and put one end of a length of plastic tubing carefully into the jar, to reach about half way down the liquid. Hold this in position and gently suck the other end of the tubing.

As the wine fills the tubing, tightly pinch the end you are sucking, and place it inside the neck of the empty fermentation jar. Release finger pressure and the wine will flow smoothly into the new container.

You must ensure that the level of wine in the jar being siphoned does not fall below the end of the tubing. Gently push the tubing further into the wine until it is impossible to draw off any more liquid without disturbing the lees.

When all the clear wine is safely inside the new fermentation jar, add a crushed Campden tablet to avoid any bacterial contamination. Top up the jar to its shoulder with a solution of sugar and water (in the same proportions as the original wine) to compensate for the amount of lees that has been discarded. Fit a clean fermentation lock.

Racking at intervals of about one month is advisable and will ensure that the wine clears rapidly.

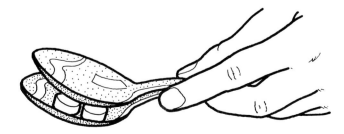

Stand the jar to be racked on a table and put in the tubing.

As the wine fills the tubing, pinch the end you are sucking.

Gently suck the other end of the tubing.

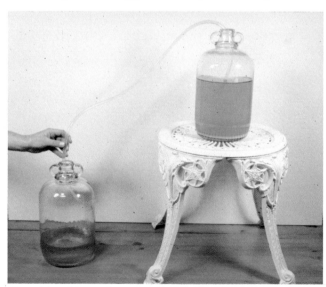

Place this end into a clean jar and release the pressure.

As the wine is siphoned off, push the tubing further down the jar.

Top up the jar to its shoulder with sugar solution.

Add a crushed Campden tablet.

Fit a clean fermentation lock.

Fining

A wine will usually clear naturally given enough time and regular racking, particularly if it is placed in a cool place when fermentation has finished.

Occasionally, however, a wine will remain persistently cloudy and you will have to try to clear it artificially. Chemical substances, known as *finings*, are available in a number of proprietary brands, and contain such ingredients as isinglass, gelatine, casein, and egg whites.

Following the manufacturer's instructions, add a small amount of finings to the wine. After a short time the wine should clear and a solid deposit will be left at the bottom of the fermentation jar. You can then rack the wine in the normal way.

Probably the best fining agent to use is *bentonite*. It is a powdered clay mineral originally formed by the alteration of volcanic rocks. To use bentonite, put some of the powder into a sterilized screw-top bottle and add a small amount of the wine to be fined. Screw on the top and shake the bottle vigorously. Leave the mixture for twenty-four hours and then add it to the wine, which will clear rapidly after treatment.

Add finings to a jar of persistently cloudy wine.

After a short time the wine should clear in the usual way.

38

Pectin haze

If wine has been made by boiling fruit or certain vegetables that contain a lot of pectin, it is possible that a haze may develop. Wines that are likely to be troublesome are best treated at the initial stages when the must is being prepared, but the fault can be rectified later by adding one of the pectin-destroying enzymes which are widely available.

Pectin is a gelatinous substance present in fruit and vegetables in varying quantities. It is of great benefit in making jam because it causes the jam to set, but it is most undesirable in winemaking because it forms a jelly-like haze, which remains in suspension after fermentation.

To avoid a pectin haze forming, or to remove one that has formed, you should treat the wine with a pectin-destroying enzyme. This enzyme is called pectinase, and it is available as either a powder or liquid, under various brand names. Follow the manufacturer's instructions to decide how much pectinase to add to your must.

Many winemakers add pectin-destroying enzyme to all fruit and vegetable wines when the mashed pulp is cool, and before sugar has been added. Although pectin is present in all fruit and vegetables, some have it in large amounts and are more likely to throw hazes. The worst offenders are apricots, damsons, parsnips, peaches, plums, and potatoes.

It is easy to decide whether or not a haze is caused by pectin. Add a small amount of the wine to be tested to methylated spirit in a bottle and shake it vigorously. Leave the mixture to settle for some time. If jelly-like strings or 'blobs' have formed, the haze is the result of pectin being present in the wine.

A jelly-like haze can be tested to see if it is caused by pectin.

Add some of the wine to a bottle containing methylated spirit.

Shake the mixture vigorously.

Starch haze

Unripe apples and a few root vegetables, notably parsnips and potatoes, are liable to produce a starch haze in the fermented wine if they are boiled too violently. If this haze does not clear when the wine has been kept in a cold position for some time, you should use a starch-destroying enzyme, called *amylase* and which, like pectinase comes in powder form and should be added to the must according to the manufacturer's instructions.

Filtering

Filtering will not remove pectin or starch hazes, but it can be considered as a last resort for an obstinately cloudy wine.

A filter paper, folded to fit into a funnel may be used although modern filter kits are better because they are air-tight and avoid the possibility of the wine becoming *oxidized*.

Wine is passed through the filtering system, and the filter paper, or pad, removes even the most minute particles of unwanted material. The filtering medium should be changed regularly to prevent it becoming blocked.

The jelly-like blobs show that pectin is present in the wine.

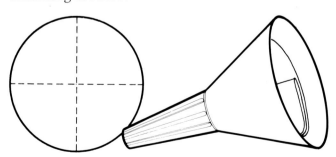

Folding a filter paper to fit inside a funnel.

A folded filter paper in a funnel may be used to clear cloudy wine.

A modern filter kit is better because it is air-tight.

Bottling, corking, and labelling

When the wine has been racked several times and is crystal clear, it is ready to be bottled. Proper wine bottles should always be used because they are strong enough to withstand the pressure caused by an unexpected refermentation after bottling. Spirit bottles are not suitable because they are made of thinner glass than wine bottles and are, therefore, more likely to burst if fermentation starts up again. Remember, though, that a wine that has been fermented to complete dryness will not contain any sugar and consequently will not referment.

Bottles

Many people buy new wine bottles, but this is generally unnecessary because empty bottles are often readily available from many sources. Hotels and restaurants are ideal donors as their empties are usually thrown away, and most proprietors are quite willing to give a few bottles away.

Wine bottles come in a wide variety of shapes and sizes and may be punted or not. The *punt* (the indentation at the bottom) helps to prevent the disturbance of any deposits which may have formed during storage, provided the bottle is stored upright.

Red or rosé wine should be put into dark-coloured bottles, because the beautiful colour of the wine will rapidly fade if it is exposed to too much light. Clear bottles, however, are quite suitable for white wines.

Opposite: A selection of suitable bottles of both clear and coloured glass, will be needed to store the wine.

You should clean and sterilize all bottles before you use them and you should also remove old labels. Wash the bottles in hot water, and rinse them until they are perfectly clean. A bottle brush is useful, and will quickly remove all but the most stubborn stains with a gentle brushing action. A solution of washing soda in water will usually remove any discoloration inside the bottles if they are filled completely and left to soak for several hours. Badly stained bottles are more trouble than they are worth and are best thrown away.

After the clean bottles have been rinsed in cold water, they should be sterilized in a sulphite solution, drained, and the outsides dried completely before being filled with wine. You should then fill the bottles to within 1½ inches (4 cm.) of the top of the bottle.

Wash the bottles in hot water.

A bottle brush will remove most stains.

Drain and dry the bottles completely.

Sterilize the bottles in sulphite solution.

Fill the bottles to within 1½ inches (4 cm) of the top.

Corks

There are several types of corks and stoppers that may be used, but corks must not be used more than once because any cracks or splits that have been made when they are removed from previous bottles may provide pathways for bacteria.

Flanged stoppers made of plastic or cork are used when a wine is not to be stored for any length of time. They are simply pushed into place using hand pressure, and can be easily removed without a corkscrew. Although these stoppers are quick and easy to use, they cannot be relied on to provide a perfectly air-tight fit unless they are covered with one of the plastic, shrink-wrap seals which are available. These are supplied in a liquid to keep them moist, and are placed over the cork, smoothed around the mouth of the bottle, and left to dry to a hard, air-tight seal.

Ordinary cylindrical corks are effective, but must be inserted with a corking tool to obtain a perfectly tight fit. If you use corks, you should soften them first. Soak them in cold water for twenty-four hours or in hot water for half-an-hour, making sure they are submerged by placing a saucer, or similar weight, over them in the bowl of water. After you have softened the corks, you should sterilize them with sulphite solution.

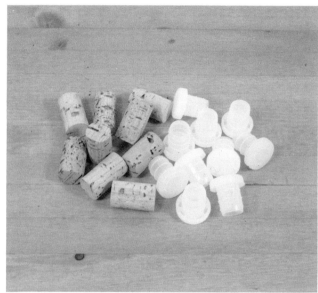

Suitable corks and stoppers.

Press flanged stoppers into place by hand.

45

Corking tools

The cheapest and most basic corking tool is a flogger. This is a wooden device which fits snugly over the mouth of a bottle. It has a hollow centre which allows the cork to pass down it under pressure. A cork is placed in the central cylinder and the plunger is hit with a mallet to force the cork down the gently narrowing tube and into the bottle, sealing it tightly. It is a good idea to put a piece of sterilized wire or string between the cork and the bottle neck to allow air to escape or the cork might be pushed out again by compressed air. Don't forget to remove the string after the cork has been forced home and the air has escaped.

More sophisticated corking machines are available, ranging from small, lever-operated hand

Cover the stoppers with shrink-wrap seals.

Soak corks for twenty-four hours, making sure they are submerged.

A flogger is a simple device for inserting corks.

46

tools, to large bench models with a production-line capacity. These are based on the same principles as the flogger, but are designed to be operated easily and with consistent results.

Whichever corking method you use, make sure that the cork is inserted so that its top is flush with the mouth of the bottle.

Finishing the bottle

Having corked the bottle it is a simple procedure to finish it off neatly, with a cover over the cork and an attractive label giving details of the type of wine and date of bottling.

Capsules of coloured metal foil or plastic may be placed over the mouth of the bottle, hiding the cork and producing a professional-looking result.

Labels are produced in a great variety of styles, and an appropriate design can be chosen to suit the type of wine, or your personal preference. If you are artistic you may wish to design and produce your own labels, giving a highly individual look to your bottles.

By taking a little trouble to ensure that the label is neatly positioned, avoiding the seams, and in the centre of the bottle, a most attractive appearance can be obtained, of which you may be justifiably proud.

Remove the sterilized string when the cork is in place.

A lever-operated corking tool makes corking simple.

Capsules of coloured foil or plastic give a professional finish.

Stick on label to record the type of wine and date.

Storing and blending your wines

When the finished wine has been bottled and labelled, it is ready to be stored until it has *matured* sufficiently to be at its best for drinking.

Bottles that have been sealed with a cork should be stored on their sides, either lying flat or at an angle, so that the cork remains in contact with the wine, and is kept moist. This ensures that the cork does not dry out and shrink permitting air to reach the wine through its minute pores.

A bottle rack is the ideal storage system for wine bottles, and these provide a neat, space-saving solution to the problem of building up a stock of maturing wine. There are several types of specially designed bottle racks, ranging from cheap plastic-coated wine stands to expensive wood and metal models.

If you do not wish to buy a purpose-made wine rack you can make do quite successfully by using cardboard bottle cartons, from your local off-licence. When placed on their sides, these become most effective bottle racks, and new cartons can be added as the need arises.

If you think it is possible that a wine may throw a deposit you should use punted bottles and store them standing upright. Any sediment that does form will be held by the punt, and will not be disturbed when the wine is poured.

The ideal place for storing wine is in a wine cellar, but these are not often readily available and you must find an alternative situation. Wine should be kept in the dark as far as possible, and at a cool, even temperature of about 13°C (55°F). The wine rack should also be placed where it is free from vibration and where it can be left undisturbed until the wine is ready for drinking.

Cardboard bottle cartons make useful bottle racks.

Punted bottles can be stored upright to collect any sediment.

If you are making large quantities of wine, you may wish to keep it in fermentation jars rather than in bottles. Jars full of maturing wine can often be conveniently stored in a cool shed, or outhouse.

Resist the temptation to drink your wine as soon as it has been bottled. You must leave it for several months at least to ensure that it is fully mature. An immature wine will taste harsh, often with an unpleasant flavour, and will not be the joy to drink that it should be.

Fermentation jars are useful to store large quantities of wine.

Blending

Occasionally a wine will taste less than perfect, even though you may have devoted great care to it. This may be a matter of personal taste, or due to some peculiarity of the initial ingredients.

As long as the wine itself is not faulty, all is not lost, because careful blending with another wine may produce a mixture that is pleasant to drink. To achieve the best results you may need to experiment with various combinations of wine. Many enjoyable hours can be spent trying various permutations. It is often most successful to blend wines of opposite characteristics; for example, a too-sweet and too-dry wine will mix to produce a wine of the right sweetness.

Blending two or more wines together may present some problems, and you should expect possible chemical changes, resulting in deposits forming, or fermentation starting up again. The advantages of blending usually outweigh the disadvantages, however, as long as the problems are acknowledged and corrected if they occur.

Finally, you should remember that a wine which is faulty in some basic way cannot be improved by blending. The only certain result of mixing an unsound wine with a good one is that the good one will be ruined.

It is unlikely that a 50/50 mixture of two wines of complementary character will produce the perfect balance so you should try several different combinations using only about a wineglassful of each before you blend the bulk. You should then sterilize the blend with a Campden tablet and leave it under fermentation lock for a month before bottling.

Wines from concentrates and canned fruit

Wines from concentrates

Much of the fun of home winemaking comes from gathering wild fruits or flowers from the fields and hedgerows, which will later become delicious drinks. Collecting and preparing the ingredients can be an enjoyable family pastime, resulting in a great feeling of achievement when the finished wine is tasted and found to be as good as a commercially prepared bottle.

Many people, however, live a long way from the abundant harvest of the countryside, or have too little spare time to be able to collect their own wild ingredients, and seek an easier way of producing their own homemade wine.

Grape juice concentrates are becoming increasingly popular with people who require a quick, trouble-free method of winemaking. Wines made from concentrates are excellent, and can be relied on to give consistent results.

Concentrates are usually made from the surplus grape harvest of continental and other wine-producing countries. Skilful blending by manufacturers allows the amateur to make Beaujolais, Bordeaux, burgundy, Chablis, claret, hock, Liebfraumilch, Moselle, Riesling, and Sauternes-type wines among others. Also available are several blends of fruit and grape juice concentrates which offer such flavours as bilberry, elderberry, cherry, and gooseberry.

The major manufacturers ensure that their cans of concentrate include everything that is required to make a gallon of wine, except for water, sugar and yeast. The work involved in getting fermentation under way is minimal, the resulting wine is quick to mature, and is often ready to drink within a few months.

Full instructions are supplied with each can, and they can either be followed exactly or adapted to suit personal tastes. The more advanced winemaker will probably wish to check the initial specific gravity of the concentrate and water mixture before adding any sugar. The dryness or sweetness of the finished wine may be considered and the must can be adjusted to give a particular alcoholic strength, if required.

Making wine from concentrates

The exact procedure for making wine from a wine concentrate varies greatly for the different brands so only very general instructions are included here.

Open the can of grape juice concentrate of your choice and pour the syrupy liquid into a clear, sterilized fermentation jar. Rinse out the can with warm water and add this to the fermentation jar. Fill up the jar, with water, to the specified amount and stir in the recommended quantities of sugar and yeast. Fit a fermentation lock and stand the jar in a warm place while the must ferments.

When carbon dioxide no longer bubbles through the fermentation lock and the specific gravity approaches 1·000 showing that fermentation has ceased and the wine begins to clear, rack the liquid from the lees, adding a Campden tablet to prevent bacterial damage or oxidation. Keep the wine in a cool place for two or more months so that it matures, and then bottle.

Opposite: Canned grape juice concentrates and canned fruit can be used to make a variety of delicious wines.

The wine will be ready to drink sooner than wine made from fresh ingredients as the instructions on the can of concentrate will indicate, but it is advisable to wait two or three more months so that it is mature and free of any harsh flavours.

Fill up with the specified amount of water.

Pour the grape juice concentrate into a fermentation jar.

Stir in the recommended quantities of sugar and yeast.

Fit a fermentation lock.

When fermentation ceases rack off the clear wine.

Wines from canned fruits

An alternative to making wine from grape juice concentrate is to use the enormous range of ordinary canned fruits available from the shops and supermarkets. There is a very wide choice of flavours, and delicious wines can be made with little effort.

Remember that most canned fruits have been heated at some stage of their manufacture, and pectin is likely to be present. This will cause a troublesome haze unless you add a teaspoonful of a pectin-destroying enzyme to the must. Canned fruits are usually supplied in a sweet syrup to preserve them, so slightly less sugar than usual is needed. There is often enough acid present to ensure good fermentation, but it is wise to taste the fruit and syrup, or to check it with *p*H paper, and to add some citric acid if it is required.

Wine made from canned fruit may be rather thin and watery unless something is added to give it body or *vinosity*, as it is called. Raisins or sultanas are ideal because these improve the vinosity and character of the wine.

Making wine from canned fruit

The following method can be regarded as standard to make one gallon (4·5 l) of wine from a 15 oz (440 g) can of fruit.

Open the can of fruit and strain off the syrup, saving this until later. Put the fruit into a fermentation bin and mash it well, adding ½ lb (225 g) of chopped raisins.

Dissolve 1 lb (450 g) of sugar in 6 pints (3·4 l) of boiling water and pour it over the fruit. Cover and leave it to cool. When it is cool add the syrup from the can together with a teaspoonful of pectin-destroying enzyme, a sachet of wine yeast, a teaspoonful of yeast nutrient, ½ teaspoonful of tannin, citric acid if the *p*H is greater than 4, and a Campden tablet. Cover and ferment the must for four days, stirring daily.

Strain the pulp through a fine sieve, gently pressing the fruit to obtain as much of the liquid as possible. Dissolve another 1 lb (450 g) of sugar in 1 pint (0·56 l) of boiling water and add this to the must. Pour the must into a fermentation jar, fit a fermentation lock securely, and allow it to ferment in the normal way. When the bubbling in the fermentation lock has slowed to a standstill, after about three weeks, and the wine has begun to clear, check that the S.G. is close to 1·000 showing that fermentation has finished. Then rack the clear wine off the lees into a clean fermentation jar and add a Campden tablet. Store it for several months, racking as necessary, and bottle the wine when it is perfectly clear. It is a good idea to leave your wine for another three months at least before drinking it.

Pie fillings can be made into wine by this method and, as they are usually already pulped, they can be put into the fermentation bin without the need for mashing.

Fruit juices, either canned or bottled, also provide a labour-saving way of producing wine. These can be poured straight into a fermentation jar with the other ingredients, and fermentation started immediately. Again it is advisable to put in some raisins to add body to the wine. Yeast, nutrient, tannin, and sugar will be required in the same proportions as with canned fruit.

Mash the fruit well in a fermentation bin.

Add chopped raisins.

Pour sugar solution over the fruit, cover and leave to cool.

Cover the bin and leave to ferment for four days.

Add the syrup, pectolytic enzyme, yeast, nutrient and tannin.

Strain the pulp through a fine sieve.

Opposite: With a little care and patience, delicious sparkling wines can be made from many ingredients.

Add more sugar solution.

Fit a fermentation lock, and leave to ferment to a finish.

Pour the must into a clean fermentation jar.

Take a hydrometer reading to check that the S.G. is near 1·000.

Sparkling wine

Delicious sparkling wines can be made from many ingredients but the best are probably apples, pears, grapes, gooseberries, and rhubarb, although some darker fruits will make attractive pink or red variations.

Firstly, produce a wine from the chosen ingredients in the normal manner, ensuring that you do not add too much sugar to the must—2½ lb (1·1 kg) per gallon (4·5 l) is about right—and this should give an initial hydrometer reading of between 1·080 and 1·086. By way of example, let us look at the method for making a sparkling apple wine. Chop 4½ lb (2 kg) of apples into small pieces and put them into a fermentation bin with ½ lb (225 g) of chopped raisins. Pour 4 pints (2·25 l) of cold water over the fruit. Dissolve 2½ lb (1·1 kg) of sugar in 3 pints (1·7 l) of boiling water, add it to the pulp, and leave it to cool. When it is lukewarm, add the grated rind and the juice of 1 lemon, a teaspoonful of pectin-destroying enzyme, a sachet of wine yeast, and a teaspoonful of vitaminized yeast nutrient. Finally, add a Campden tablet, cover the bin securely, and leave the must to ferment for eight or nine days, stirring and mashing the pulp daily. Strain the liquid off through a fine-mesh straining bag into a fermentation jar, top up with cold water, and fit a fermentation lock. Put the jar in a warm place until fermentation is complete and the wine begins to clear.

Ferment the wine until all the sugar has been used up and a dry wine has been produced. Rack the wine at suitable intervals until it is perfectly clear. If necessary, add finings, or filter the wine to remove any haze. Then leave the wine to mature for about six months.

After this time, dissolve 2½ oz (70 g) of sugar in each gallon (4·5 l) of the wine. Prepare a champagne yeast in a starter bottle using ½ pint (0·5 l) of fruit juice, 1 oz (28 g) of sugar, a pinch of citric acid, and a pinch of nutrient and, when it is fermenting vigorously, add it to the wine and seal the jar with a fermentation lock. Champagne yeasts have been specially developed to produce the desired flavour and to throw a firm sediment, so always use these rather than an ordinary wine yeast which may be difficult to clear and liable to spoil your sparkling wine.

Clean and sterilize some champagne bottles to store the wine in. It is absolutely essential to use proper champagne bottles, because only these are strong enough to withstand the high pressure of carbon dioxide gas formed by wine undergoing fermentation. Always use sound bottles, discarding any that are chipped or weakened in any way. An exploding bottle could be extremely dangerous, and all sensible precautions should be taken to avoid it occurring.

When the wine is fermenting thoroughly, siphon it into the bottles, filling them to 2 inches (5 cm) below the mouth of each bottle. Seal them with a hollow plastic stopper and place a wire cage, called a *muselet*, over each stopper, tightening them firmly over the mouth of the bottle. Label the bottles making sure that you record the date of the secondary fermentation as well as the date you did the bottling.

Put the chopped fruit into a fermentation bin.

Add the remaining ingredients and a Campden tablet.

Dissolve the sugar in boiling water.

Cover the bin securely and leave to ferment for several days.

Strain the liquid into a fermentation jar.

Rack the wine at intervals until it is perfectly clear.

Top up with cold water and fit a fermentation lock.

Dissolve 2½ oz (70 g) of sugar in each gallon (4.5 l) of wine.

Prepare a champagne yeast in a starter bottle.

When the wine is fermenting, siphon it into champagne bottles.

Add the yeast starter to the wine and fit a fermentation lock.

Seal the bottles with hollow stoppers and wire cages.

Stick on labels and record the date of bottling.

Store upside down so that any sediment collects in the stoppers.

Put the bottles in a warm place for about a week so that fermentation will proceed well, and then move them to a cool position where they can be stored for several months or a year if possible. During this period the bottles should be kept upside down, so that the yeast deposit that forms from the fermentation is collected inside the hollow stopper. Plastic stoppers are now available with a short tube sticking out from the flat top. This allows sediment to pass through the hollow stopper to be collected in the tube. The tube is cut off to remove the deposits, before the wine is served.

When the wine is ready for serving, place the neck of the bottle into some crushed ice until the sediment inside the hollow stopper has frozen. Remove the wire cage and ease out the stopper, holding the bottle horizontally until the moment the stopper, containing the frozen sediment, pops out.

The secondary fermentation will have used up all of the sugar, and the sparkling wine will, therefore, be very dry. To overcome this the wine may be sweetened with either one saccharin tablet to each bottle, or a solution of 1 lb (450 g) caster sugar dissolved in 1 pint (0·56 l) of wine and added to suit individual taste.

After sweetening, seal the bottle again with a clean stopper and rewire it until the wine is required, perhaps an hour or so later. Serve the sparkling wine at a temperature of about 45°F (8°C).

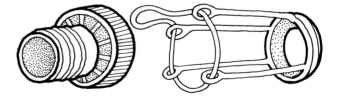

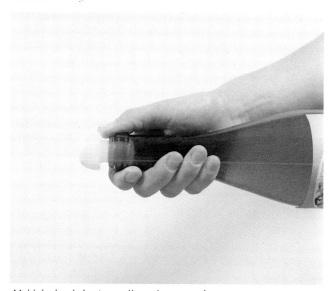

Place the neck of the bottle into some crushed ice.

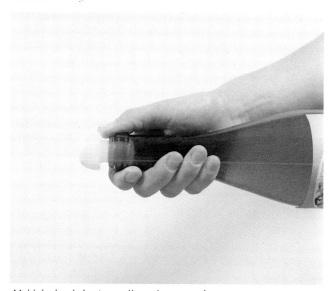

Hold the bottle horizontally and ease out the stopper.

Malolactic fermentation

Sometimes an ordinary wine a year or more old will accidentally become sparkling. This is caused by a malolactic fermentation which is usually the result of not using enough Campden tablets to destroy all the bacteria present.

Many fruits contain malic acid, and this can be converted into lactic acid and carbon dioxide by a micro-organism. The result of this reaction is that the wine becomes less sharp and slightly sparkling. Although a pleasant-tasting wine may be produced by malolactic fermentation, you should not try to encourage such quirks of fate. It is more likely that harmful bacteria will flourish if you do not use enough Campden tablets, and your wine will be ruined.

Mead

Mead is probably one of the most ancient alcoholic drinks, and is known to have been produced for many thousands of years although its origins are uncertain.

Basically, it is made from honey and water although many additives may be introduced to produce different flavours. Herbs and spices are often added, but many other ingredients such as fruits or juices may be used to obtain different results.

Many types of honey are used to make mead of individual characteristics. Light honey will make an excellent dry white mead, while darker honey is best used to produce sweet or spiced mead. Pure English honey is difficult to beat, and its quality is well worth its extra cost.

Remember that honey is often inconsistent in taste, depending upon the sort of nectar that the honeybees have been feeding on. Bees collecting pollen from orange blossom will make a honey of quite different taste and quality to that made by bees using a clover field as their source of supply.

Honey is about 75 per cent sugar together with water, mineral salts, and trace elements. Because honey is so sweet, you do not need to add sugar to make mead, and you will need 3 lb (1·3 kg) of honey per gallon (4·5 l) to produce a dry mead, or 4 lb (1·8 kg) per gallon (4·5 l) for a sweet mead.

For fermentation to take place it is essential to add acid, tannin, and yeast nutrient, because honey does not have enough of these in itself.

Making mead

Honey is likely to contain unwanted bacteria and these must be removed by sterilization to make sure that the mead does not become infected or turn to vinegar. There are two ways of sterilizing the honey.

Empty the quantity of honey required for either a sweet or dry mead into the fermentation bin. Boil 1 gallon (4·5 l) of water and pour it over the honey in the bin, stirring until all the honey has dissolved. When the liquid is lukewarm, add two Campden tablets to each gallon (4·5 l) of honey and water solution. Alternatively, you can mix the honey with hot water until it dissolves and then boil the liquid for a few moments to sterilize it. This method will kill off any harmful organisms and will also form a scum of wax and other unwanted material on the top of the liquid which can be skimmed off carefully and discarded.

To the lukewarm solution, add about ½ oz (15 g) of citric acid and check the *p*H with acidity paper —it should be between *p*H 3 and 4. Add a teaspoonful of grape tannin, a teaspoonful of vitaminized yeast nutrient, and a sachet of mead yeast or a good wine yeast that will throw a sediment readily.

Pour the liquid into a fermentation jar and put it in a warm place for fermentation to proceed. When the wine ceases bubbling and begins to clear, check that the S.G. is close to 1·000, and then rack the wine into a clean fermentation jar and add a Campden tablet. As sediment forms you should rack it again until the wine drops perfectly clear. Mead should be left to mature for at least six months before it is bottled. After that the mead should be left for at least another three months before drinking, and preferably longer.

A sparkling mead can be made by adding a champagne yeast to the finished wine, and refermenting in the bottle, following the method described for ordinary wine starting on page 25.

Crush two Campden tablets and add them to the mixture.

Pour boiling water over the honey in a fermentation bin.

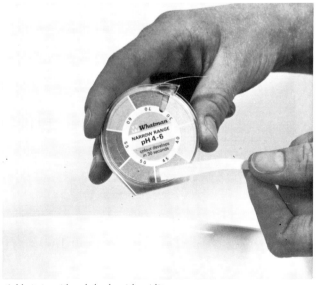
Add citric acid and check with acidity paper.

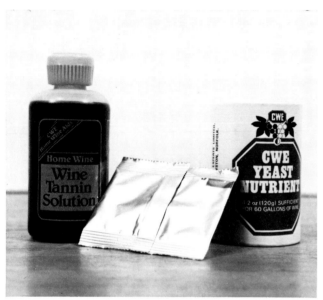

Add tannin, yeast nutrient and mead yeast.

When fermentation ceases check that the S.G. is close to 1·000.

Pour the liquid into a fermentation jar and fit a lock.

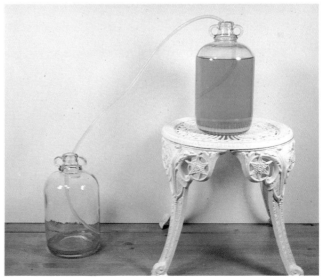

Rack the mead into a clean fermentation jar.

Weights, measures, & their abbreviations

The use of weights and measures in Britain continues to be in a state of confusion although more and more products are now sold in metric quantities. In winemaking you will often find that vessels are marked in both Imperial and in metric units although fermentation jars still seem to be mainly of the 1 gallon volume. In this book, Imperial measures have always been given first and their exact metric equivalents given afterwards in brackets. You may find, however, that you will wish to round up or down these figures in the metric system so that, for example, you use 5 litres of liquid rather than 4·54 litres which is the exact conversion of 1 gallon.

The following conversion table which also gives the abbreviations that have been used in this book should help you.

1 pound (lb)	0·45 kilograms (kg)
1 ounce (oz)	28 grams (g)
1 gallon	4·54 litres (l)
1 pint	0·56 litres (l)
teaspoonful (tsp)	
tablespoonful (tbsp)	

To convert temperature from degrees Fahrenheit to degrees Centigrade, subtract 32° from the Fahrenheit, multiply by 5, and divide by 9. To convert from Centigrade to Fahrenheit multiply by 9, divide by 5, and add 32°.

Whichever system you use, stick to it and do not mix the two systems.

Picking wild plants

A number of wild plants are specifically protected by law and may not be picked. Although none of these plants are normally used for winemaking it is worth remembering that the Wildlife and Countryside Act 1981 states that it is an offence for any unauthorised person to uproot any wild plant.

Nobody will mind you picking the leaves and flowers of the more common plants and 'weeds', but a little common sense and consideration should be shown when gathering ingredients from the countryside.

Commercially dried and prepared flowers are often available from home winemaking retailers, and these make a sensible alternative to picking your own.

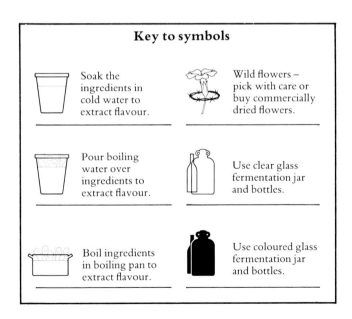

Key to symbols

Soak the ingredients in cold water to extract flavour.

Wild flowers – pick with care or buy commercially dried flowers.

Pour boiling water over ingredients to extract flavour.

Use clear glass fermentation jar and bottles.

Boil ingredients in boiling pan to extract flavour.

Use coloured glass fermentation jar and bottles.

Poison—not to be taken

It is unfortunate that the uninformed gatherer of wild flowers and berries runs the risk of picking ingredients which may be poisonous to a greater or lesser degree. You should, therefore, study suitable guides which describe and illustrate poisonous plants so that you can avoid them.

Several plants are highly toxic and can prove fatal if swallowed even in relatively small amounts. Other plants should also be avoided because they are poisonous or unpleasant, in varying degrees. Although the process of fermentation may neutralize some poisonous substances in certain circumstances, it is unwise to assume that this is often the case and any doubtful ingredients should be discarded.

The following list gives some of the more common poisonous plants, but by no means all of them. Uncertainty about a particular plant, flower, or berry is good enough reason not to use it.

Poisonous plants

aconite
alder
anemone
aquilegia
azalea
baneberry
berberis
black nightshade
bluebell
bryony
broom
buckthorn buttercup

celandine
charlock
clematis
columbine
cowbane
crocus
chrysanthemum
cuckoo pint
cyclamen
daffodil
dahlia
deadly nightshade

delphinium
dwarf elder
fool's parsley
figwort
foxglove
geranium
gladiolus
green potatoes
hellebore family
hemlock
henbane
holly
honeysuckle
horse chestnut
hyacinth
iris
ivy
jasmin
jonquil
laburnum
laurel
lilac
lily-of-the-valley
lily
lobelia
lucerne
lupin

marsh marigold
meadow rue
mezereon
mistletoe
monkshood
narcissus
orchids
pheasant's eye
peony
poppy
privet
ragwort
rhododendron
rhubarb leaves
snowdrop
spearwort
spindleberry
spurge
sweet pea
thorn apple
tomato stems and leaves
traveller's joy
tulip
wood anemone
woody nightshade
yew

Spring recipes

Apricot Wine

canned apricots	15½ oz	·5 kg
sugar	2 lb	1 kg
water	1 gallon	4·5 l
chopped raisins	½ lb	225 g
citric acid	2 tsp	2 tsp
pectin-destroying enzyme	1 tsp	1 tsp
yeast and yeast nutrient	sachet	sachet
	and 1 tsp	and 1 tsp
tannin	½ tsp	½ tsp
Campden tablets		

Open the can and strain off the syrup, saving it until later. Put the apricots into a fermentation bin and mash them well, then add the raisins. Dissolve 1 lb (450 g) of sugar in 6 pints (3·4 l) of boiling water and pour it over the fruit. Cover and leave to cool. Then add the syrup together with some pectin-destroying enzyme, yeast, yeast nutrient, acid, tannin, and a Campden tablet. Cover and ferment the must for four days, stirring daily.

Strain the liquid through a fine-mesh bag into a clean fermentation jar. Dissolve another 1 lb (450 g) of sugar in a pint (0·56 l) of boiling water and add it to the must. Pour it all into a fermentation jar and top up with water, fit a fermentation lock containing sterilizing solution and ferment in a warm place.

When fermentation has finished, the bubbling has ceased, and the wine has started to clear, check that the S.G. is close to 1·000, rack the clear wine into another jar, add a Campden tablet, and bottle when the wine is perfectly clear. Your wine should be ready to drink after three months.

Balm Wine

balm leaves	2 quarts	2 l
sugar	2½ lb	1·1 kg
water	1 gallon	4·5 l
chopped raisins	1 lb	450 g
orange	1	1
large lemons	2	2
yeast and yeast nutrient	1 sachet and 1 tsp	1 sachet and 1 tsp
tannin	1 tsp	1 tsp
Campden tablets		

Put the balm leaves into a fermentation bin together with the grated rinds of the orange and lemons. Boil the water and pour it over the leaves. Cover and allow to cool before adding the orange and lemon juice and a Campden tablet. Leave the mixture for two or three days, stirring daily.

Strain off the liquid through a fine-mesh bag into another fermentation vessel, and stir in the sugar until it has dissolved. Add the raisins, yeast, yeast nutrient, and tannin, and cover securely. Let the liquid ferment for six days, stirring well each day.

Strain the must into a fermentation jar, insert a fermentation lock containing sterilizing solution and put the jar in a warm place so that fermentation continues.

When fermentation has ceased, the bubbling has stopped, and the wine clears, check that the S.G. is near 1·000, rack it into another jar and add a Campden tablet. Rack it again after a couple of months, and bottle when it is perfectly clear. It should be ready to drink in six to nine months.

Clover mead

clover honey	4 lb	2 kg
water	1 gallon	4·5 l
citric acid	½ oz	15 g
mead yeast and yeast nutrient	1 sachet and 1 tsp	1 sachet and 1 tsp
tannin	1 tsp	1 tsp
Campden tablets		

Empty the honey into a fermentation bin, boil the water and pour it over, stirring until the honey has dissolved. Cover and leave to cool. When lukewarm add the acid, yeast, yeast nutrient, tannin and two Campden tablets. Pour the liquid into a fermentation jar, insert a fermentation lock containing sterilizing solution, and put it in a warm place for fermentation to proceed.

When fermentation has finished, the bubbling has stopped, the S.G. is close to 1·000, and the wine clears, rack into a clean fermentation jar and add a Campden tablet. Rack again, at suitable intervals, as sediment forms, and leave to mature for at least six months before bottling. Do not be tempted to drink it for another three months.

Clover wine

red clover flower heads	2 quarts	2 kg
sugar	2½ lb	1·1 kg
water	1 gallon	4·5 l
chopped raisins	½ lb	225 g
citric acid	2 tsp	2 tsp
yeast and yeast nutrient	1 sachet and 1 tsp	1 sachet and 1 tsp
tannin	1 tsp	1 tsp
Campden tablets		

Put the flower heads into a fermentation bin, together with the raisins. Boil the water, pour it over, cover, and leave to cool. When lukewarm, add a Campden tablet, cover again and leave to soak for three or four days, stirring daily.

Strain the liquid through a fine-mesh bag into a clean vessel and add the sugar, stirring until it dissolves. Add the acid, yeast, yeast nutrient and tannin. Stir well, then pour the must into a fermentation jar and fit a fermentation lock containing sterilizing solution. Put the jar in a warm place to ferment to a finish, when the bubbling stops, the wine begins to clear, and the S.G. is close to 1·000.

Rack the clear wine into a clean fermentation jar and add a Campden tablet. Repeat the racking until the wine is perfectly clear, then bottle and store for several months before serving.

Coltsfoot wine

coltsfoot flowers	1 gallon	4·5 l
sugar	2½ lb	1·1 kg
water	1 gallon	4·5 l
orange	1	1
large lemons	2	2
yeast and yeast nutrient	1 sachet and 1 tsp	1 sachet and 1 tsp
tannin	1 tsp	1 tsp
Campden tablets		

Put the bright-yellow flowers into a fermentation bin with the grated rind of the orange and lemons. Boil the water and pour it over the flowers. Cover and leave to cool. Then add the orange and lemon juice and a Campden tablet. Cover and leave for three or four days, stirring daily.

Strain the liquid through a fine-mesh bag, into another fermentation bin and stir in the sugar. Add the yeast, yeast nutrient, and tannin, and cover well. Leave the mixture to soak for four or five days and stir thoroughly each day.

Strain the must into a fermentation jar, fit a fermentation lock containing sterilizing solution and put the jar in a warm place to continue fermenting to a finish when the bubbling stops, the wine begins to clear, and the S.G. is close to 1·000.

When fermentation has finished, rack off the clear liquid and add a Campden tablet. Rack again, as required, until the wine is perfectly clear and then bottle. Leave the wine for six to nine months before drinking.

Cowslip wine

cowslip flowers	1 gallon	4·5 l
sugar	2½ lb	1·1 kg
water	1 gallon	4·5 l
orange	1	1
large lemons	2	2
yeast and yeast nutrient	1 sachet and 1 tsp	1 sachet and 1 tsp
tannin	1 tsp	1 tsp
Campden tablets		

Remove all green stems and lower parts of the flowers and place the flowers in a fermentation bin together with the grated rinds of the orange and lemons. Boil the water, pour it over the flowers, cover and leave to cool. Add the orange and lemon juice and a Campden tablet. Cover and leave for three or four days, stirring daily.

Then strain the liquid through a fine-mesh bag into a clean fermentation bin and add the sugar, stirring until it has dissolved. Put in the yeast, yeast nutrient, and tannin. Cover securely and leave to ferment for five or six days, stirring daily.

Strain the liquid through a fine-mesh bag into a fermentation jar. Fit a fermentation lock containing sterilizing solution and put the jar in a warm place to ferment until the bubbling stops, the wine begins to clear, and the S.G. is close to 1·000.

Rack off the clear liquid when fermentation has finished and put it into a clean jar. Add a Campden tablet and leave to clear completely. Store the wine for a few months before bottling. Then leave it for a further six months before drinking.

Currant wine

currants (dried)	3 lb	1·5 kg
sugar	2½ lb	1·1 kg
water	1 gallon	4·5 l
oranges	2	2
large lemons	2	2
pectin-destroying enzyme	1 tsp	1 tsp
yeast and yeast nutrient	1 sachet and 1 tsp	1 sachet and 1 tsp
tannin	1 tsp	1 tsp
Campden tablets		

Chop the currants thoroughly and put them into a fermentation bin with the sugar. Boil the water and pour it over the currants and sugar, stirring to dissolve the sugar. Cover and let the mixture cool. Then add the grated rind and juice of the oranges and lemons, pectin-destroying enzyme, yeast, yeast nutrient, and tannin. Cover securely and allow to ferment for five or six days, stirring the mixture each day.

Strain the liquid through a fine-mesh bag into a fermentation jar and fit a fermentation lock containing sterilizing solution. Continue the fermentation in a warm place and allow to finish so that the bubbling has stopped, the wine begins to clear, and the S.G. is close to 1·000.

As the wine clears, rack it into a clean fermentation jar, and add a Campden tablet. Rack again, if necessary, and bottle the wine when it is perfectly clear. Keep the wine for three to six months before drinking.

Dandelion wine

dandelion heads	2 quarts	2 l
sugar	2½ lb	1·1 kg
water	1 gallon	4·5 l
chopped raisins	1 lb	450 g
orange	1	1
large lemons	2	2
yeast and yeast nutrient	1 sachet and 1 tsp	1 sachet and 1 tsp
tannin	1 tsp	1 tsp
Campden tablets		

Use fresh dandelion heads, discarding as much green as possible, and put them into a fermentation bin with the grated rind of the oranges and lemons. Boil the water and pour it over the heads. Cover and leave to cool. Then add the orange and lemon juice and a Campden tablet. Cover and leave for two or three days, stirring daily.

Strain off the liquid through a fine-mesh bag into another fermentation bin and add the raisins, tannin, sugar, yeast, and yeast nutrient. Cover well and leave to ferment for six days, stirring each day.

Strain the must into a fermentation jar, fit a fermentation lock containing sterilizing solution, and put the jar in a warm place to ferment.

When fermentation has ceased, the bubbling has stopped, the wine begins to clear, and the S.G. is close to 1·000, rack off the clear liquid and add a Campden tablet. Rack again, as necessary, until the wine is perfectly clear, and store for several months to mature before bottling. Leave for nine months to a year before drinking.

Elderflower wine

elderflowers	1 pint	·5 l
sugar	2½ lb	1·1 kg
water	1 gallon	4·5 l
large lemons	3	3
yeast and yeast nutrient	1 sachet and 1 tsp	1 sachet and 1 tsp
tannin	1 tsp	1 tsp
Campden tablets		

Put the elderflower heads into a fermentation bin together with the grated rinds of the lemons. Boil the water and pour it over the flowers. Cover the bin and leave to cool. Add a Campden tablet and leave to soak for two or three days, stirring daily.

Strain the liquid off through a fine-mesh bag into another clean fermentation vessel and add the juice of the lemons. Add the sugar, making sure it dissolves, and then put in the yeast, yeast nutrient, and tannin. Cover securely and leave to ferment for four or five days.

Strain the liquid off again through a fine-mesh bag and pour it into a fermentation jar. Fit a fermentation lock containing sterilizing solution and put the jar in a warm place for fermentation to continue. When fermentation has finished, the bubbling will stop, the wine will begin to clear, and the S.G. should be near 1·000.

Rack the clear liquid off the lees and put it in a clean fermentation jar, adding a Campden tablet. If another sediment is thrown rack it again until the wine is perfectly clear, and then bottle. Leave it for six to nine months before drinking.

Gooseberry wine

green gooseberries	6 lb	2·75 kg
sugar	2½ lb	1·1 kg
water	1 gallon	4·5 l
citric acid	1 tsp	5 g
yeast and yeast nutrient	1 sachet and 1 tsp	1 sachet and 1 tsp
pectin-destroying enzyme	1 tsp	1 tsp
tannin	1 tsp	1 tsp
Campden tablets		

Wash and top-and-tail the gooseberries. Put them into a fermentation bin and squeeze them by hand. Boil the water and pour it over them, cover and leave to cool. Then add the pectin-destroying enzyme and a Campden tablet. Cover again and leave to soak for three days, stirring daily.

Strain off the liquid through a fine-mesh bag into another fermentation vessel. Test the acidity and add some citric acid if necessary. Add the sugar, stirring until it has dissolved. Stir in the yeast, yeast nutrient, and tannin, cover securely and allow to ferment for four days.

Strain the liquid through a fine-mesh bag again, and pour it into a fermentation jar, topping up with water if required. Fit a fermentation lock containing sterilizing solution and leave in a warm place to ferment. When fermentation has ceased, bubbling has stopped, the wine begins to clear, and the S.G. is close to 1·000 rack into a clean jar and add a Campden tablet. Rack the wine again as it clears, and let the wine mature for several months before bottling. Leave it for a year before drinking.

Hawthorn blossom wine

hawthorn blossom	2 quarts	2 l
sugar	2½ lb	1·1 kg
water	1 gallon	4·5 l
orange	1	1
large lemons	2	2
yeast and yeast nutrient	1 sachet and 1 tsp	1 sachet and 1 tsp
tannin	1 tsp	1 tsp
Campden tablets		

Remove any pieces of leaf or stalk and put the flowers into a fermentation bin with the grated rind of the orange and lemons. Boil the water and pour it over the blossom. Cover the bin. When the liquid is cool, add the orange and lemon juice and a Campden tablet. Cover again and leave for three or four days, stirring each day.

Strain the liquid through a fine-mesh bag into a clean fermentation bin and stir in the sugar until it has dissolved. Then put in the yeast, yeast nutrient, and tannin. Cover securely and let the mixture ferment for five or six days, stirring daily.

Strain the must into a fermentation jar, fit a fermentation lock containing sterilizing solution, and put the jar in a warm place to continue fermenting until the bubbling stops, the wine begins to clear, and the S.G. is close to 1·000.

After fermentation has completely finished and the wine has cleared, rack into a clean jar, add a Campden tablet, and leave in a cool place. Rack again as necessary until the wine is perfectly clear and ready for bottling. Leave it for a further six to nine months before drinking.

Lemon thyme wine

lemon thyme leaves	1 pint	·5 l
sugar	2½ lb	1·1 kg
water	1 gallon	4·5 l
chopped raisins	1 lb	450 g
citric acid	2 tsp	2 tsp
yeast and yeast nutrient	1 sachet and 1 tsp	1 sachet and 1 tsp
tannin	1 tsp	1 tsp
Campden tablets		

Wash the lemon thyme leaves and drain them well. Then put them into a fermentation bin. Boil the water, pour it over the leaves, and add the raisins. Cover and leave for three or four days, stirring well each day.

Strain the liquid through a fine-mesh bag on to the sugar in a clean fermentation bin and stir until the sugar has dissolved. Put in the citric acid, yeast, yeast nutrient, and tannin, and cover again. Leave to ferment for five or six days, stirring daily.

Strain the must into a fermentation jar, insert a fermentation lock containing sterilizing solution, and put in a warm place so that fermentation may continue.

After some weeks fermentation will slow down and eventually stop. The wine will begin to clear and the S.G. will be close to 1·000. Rack the wine into a clean jar, add a Campden tablet, and bottle when the wine is perfectly clear. Do not drink for another six to nine months.

Lime blossom wine

lime blossom	2 quarts	2 l
sugar	2½ lb	1·1 kg
water	1 gallon	4·5 l
chopped raisins	1 lb	450 g
wheat	½ lb	225 g
citric acid	2 tsp	2 tsp
yeast and yeast nutrient	1 sachet and 1 tsp	1 sachet and 1 tsp
Campden tablets		

Put the blossom into a fermentation bin, crush with a wooden spoon, and add the wheat and raisins. Boil the water and pour it over the ingredients, mashing them well with the wooden spoon. Cover and allow to cool. Then add the acid, sugar, yeast, yeast nutrient, and tannin. Cover well and leave to ferment for four or five days, stirring daily.

Then strain the liquid through a fine-mesh bag into a fermentation jar. Top up with water if necessary, fit a fermentation lock containing sterilizing fluid, and put in a warm place to continue fermentation until the bubbling stops, the wine begins to clear, and the S.G. is close to 1·000.

When fermentation has ceased, rack the clear liquid into a clean jar and add a Campden tablet. Store for several months before bottling. If possible keep for another year before drinking.

Nettle wine

nettle tops	2 quarts	2 l
sugar	2½ lb	1·1 kg
water	1 gallon	4·5 l
bruised ginger	½ oz	10 g
large lemons	2	2
yeast and yeast nutrient	1 sachet and 1 tsp	1 sachet and 1 tsp
tannin	1 tsp	1 tsp
Campden tablets		

Use the tops of young nettles, wash them carefully and drain. Put them into a boiling pan with the grated rinds of the lemons, the bruised ginger, and half the water. Bring to the boil, then simmer for half-an-hour. Strain the liquid on to the sugar in a fermentation bin and stir until it has dissolved. Add the rest of the water, cover and leave to cool. Then add the lemon juice, yeast, yeast nutrient, and tannin. Cover well and leave to ferment for five or six days, stirring each day.

Strain the liquid off through a fine-mesh bag into a fermentation jar and fit a fermentation lock containing sterilizing solution. Leave the jar in a warm place for fermentation to continue until the bubbling stops, the wine begins to clear, and the S.G. is close to 1·000.

When fermentation has finished, rack off the clear liquid into another jar and add a Campden tablet. Rack again if a sediment forms and store for two or three months before bottling. Leave the wine for a further six to nine months before drinking.

Parsley wine

parsley	1 lb	450 g
sugar	2½ lb	1·1 kg
water	1 gallon	4·5 l
oranges	2	2
large lemons	2	2
yeast and yeast nutrient	1 sachet and 1 tsp	1 sachet and 1 tsp
tannin	1 tsp	1 tsp
Campden tablets		

Wash the parsley well and put it into a boiling pan together with the grated rinds of the oranges and lemons and the water. Bring to the boil and simmer for 15 minutes then strain the liquid on to the sugar in a fermentation bin. Stir until the sugar has dissolved, cover, and leave to cool. When lukewarm, add the orange and lemon juice, yeast, yeast nutrient, and tannin. Cover well and allow to ferment for six days, stirring daily.

Strain the liquid through a fine-mesh bag into a fermentation jar. Top up with water as required and fit a fermentation lock containing sterilizing solution. Put the jar in a warm place and leave to ferment to a finish, when the wine will stop bubbling, begin to clear, and the S.G. will be near 1·000.

When the wine clears, rack the clear liquid into another fermentation jar and add a Campden tablet. Rack again, as necessary, until the wine is perfectly clear, then bottle. Leave it for six to nine months before drinking.

Primrose wine

primrose flowers	1 gallon	4·5 l
sugar	2½ lb	1·1 kg
water	1 gallon	4·5 l
orange	1	1
large lemons	2	2
yeast and yeast nutrient	1 sachet and 1 tsp	1 sachet and 1 tsp
tannin	1 tsp	1 tsp
Campden tablets		

Boil the water and pour it over the primrose flowers and grated rind of the orange and lemons in a fermentation bin. When cool add the juice of the orange and lemons and a Campden tablet. Cover and leave to soak for three or four days, stirring daily.

Strain off the liquid through a fine-mesh bag into another fermentation vessel and add the sugar, stirring until it dissolves. Then add the yeast, yeast nutrient, and tannin. Cover securely and allow to ferment for five or six days, stirring each day, before straining the liquid into a fermentation jar. Insert a fermentation lock containing sterilizing solution and leave in a warm place to ferment fully so that the wine stops bubbling, begins to clear, and the S.G. is close to 1·000.

After fermentation has ceased, move to a cool position to allow the wine to clear. Rack every four weeks or until the wine is perfectly clear, and then bottle. The wine should be drinkable after a further three months but will improve if kept a little longer.

Raspberry jam wine

raspberry jam	3 lb	1·5 kg
sugar	1½ lb	·75 kg
water	1 gallon	4·5 l
chopped raisins	½ lb	225 g
citric acid	2 tsp	2 tsp
pectin-destroying enzyme	1 tsp	1 tsp
yeast and yeast nutrient	1 sachet and 1 tsp	1 sachet and 1 tsp
tannin	1 tsp	1 tsp
Campden tablets		

Put the jam into a fermentation bin, boil the water and pour it over. Leave to cool, and when luke-warm, add the pectin-destroying enzyme, acid, and a Campden tablet. Cover and leave for 24 hours. Then add the raisins, tannin, sugar, yeast, and yeast nutrient. Cover well and leave to ferment for four or five days, stirring each day.

Strain the liquid through a fine-mesh bag into a fermentation jar, fit a fermentation lock containing sterilizing solution, and leave in a warm place to ferment to a finish. The bubbling should stop, the wine begin to clear, and the S.G. should be close to 1·000.

Rack the clear wine off the lees into a clean jar and add a Campden tablet. Store for six months, racking again if a sediment forms, and bottle when the wine is absolutely clear. The wine should be drinkable after a further three months.

Rhubarb wine

rhubarb	6 lb	2·75 kg
sugar	2½ lb	1·1 kg
water	7 pints	4 l
yeast and yeast nutrient	1 sachet and 1 tsp	1 sachet and 1 tsp
pectin-destroying enzyme	1 tsp	1 tsp
tannin	1 tsp	1 tsp
precipitated chalk	½ oz	14 g
Campden tablets		

The rhubarb is best picked at the end of May. Remove the rhubarb leaves, wipe and cut up the stalks, and put the pieces into a fermentation bin. Boil the water and pour it over the rhubarb. Leave to cool. Then add some pectin-destroying enzyme and a Campden tablet. Cover and leave for 1 day.

Check the acidity with acidity paper and, if necessary, neutralize some of the acid with precipitated chalk to achieve a pH of 3 to 4. Add half the sugar, stirring until it dissolves, and then put in the yeast, yeast nutrient, and tannin. Cover securely and ferment for three or four days, stirring daily.

Strain off the liquid through a fine-mesh bag and add the rest of the sugar. Pour the must into a fermentation jar, fit a fermentation lock containing sterilizing solution, and put in a warm place to ferment until the bubbling stops, the wine begins to clear, and the S.G. is close to 1·000. When fermentation has finished, rack into a clean jar and add a Campden tablet. As the wine clears, rack it again, as necessary. Store for a few months in a cool place before bottling. An excellent wine for blending.

Tea wine

tea	4 tbsp	4 tbsp
sugar	2½ lb	1·1 kg
water	1 gallon	4·5 l
citric acid	2 tbsp	2 tbsp
yeast and yeast nutrient	1 sachet and 1 tsp	1 sachet and 1 tsp
Campden tablets		

Boil the water and pour it over the tea of your choice in a fermentation bin. Stir in the sugar until it dissolves. Cover and leave to cool. Then strain the liquid into a fermentation jar and add the acid, yeast, and yeast nutrient. Fit a fermentation lock containing sterilizing solution and put the jar in a warm place for fermentation to take place.

When the must has finished fermenting, the bubbling has stopped, and it has cleared, check that the S.G. is near 1·000. Then rack into a clean jar and add a Campden tablet. Rack again if a deposit forms, store for several months, and bottle when the wine is perfectly clear. This is a particularly good wine for blending.

Summer recipes

Blackcurrant wine

blackcurrants	*3 lb*	*1·5 kg*
sugar	*2½ lb*	*1·1 kg*
water	*1 gallon*	*4.5l*
pectin-destroying enzyme	*1 tsp*	*1 tsp*
yeast and yeast nutrient	*1 sachet and 1 tsp*	*1 sachet and 1 tsp*
tannin	*1 tsp*	*1 tsp*
Campden tablets		

Wash the blackcurrants, remove any stalks, and put them into a fermentation bin. Mash them well by hand and pour on 4 pints (2·25 l) of water. Stir well and add a Campden tablet. Dissolve the sugar in 3 pints (1·8 l) of water and pour this over the pulp. When the liquid is cool add the pectin-destroying enzyme, yeast, yeast nutrient, and tannin. Cover well and leave to ferment for seven days, stirring daily.

Strain the liquid through a fine-mesh bag into a fermentation jar and top up with water. Fit a fermentation lock containing sterilizing solution and put the jar in a warm place to ferment out until the bubbling stops, the wine begins to clear, and the S.G. is close to 1·000.

When fermentation has finished, rack the clear wine into a clean fermentation jar, add a Campden tablet and store for several months. Rack again if a deposit forms and bottle into dark bottles when the wine is perfectly clear. Do not drink the wine for nine months to a year.

Broad bean wine

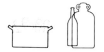

shelled broad beans	4½ lb	2 kg
sugar	2½ lb	1·1 kg
water	1 gallon	4·5 l
chopped raisins	½ lb	225 g
large lemon	1	1
yeast and yeast nutrient	1 sachet and 1 tsp	1 sachet and 1 tsp
Campden tablets		

Put the beans into a boiling pan, together with the grated rind of the lemon, and pour on the water. Bring to the boil, then simmer gently for an hour. Cover and leave to cool before straining the liquid on to the raisins, lemon juice, tannin, yeast, and yeast nutrient in a fermentation bin. Cover well and leave to ferment for four or five days, stirring daily.

Strain the liquid off through a fine-mesh bag, and stir in the sugar making sure it dissolves. Pour the liquid into a fermentation jar and insert a fermentation lock containing sterilizing solution. Put the jar in a warm place and allow to ferment to a finish so that the bubbling stops, the wine begins to clear, and the S.G. is about 1·000.

Rack the clear wine into a clean fermentation jar and add a Campden tablet. Store the wine for several months, racking at intervals if a sediment forms. Bottle when the wine is perfectly clear and mature for six to nine months.

Bullace wine

bullaces	4½ lb	2 kg
sugar	2½ lb	1·1 kg
water	1 gallon	4·5 l
chopped raisins	½ lb	225 g
pectin-destroying enzyme	1 tsp	1 tsp
yeast and yeast nutrient	1 sachet and 1 tsp	1 sachet and 1 tsp
Campden tablets		

Wash the bullaces, remove the stalks, put them into a fermentation bin, and crush them. Add the raisins, boil the water, and pour it over the fruit. Cover and leave to cool. Then remove as many stones as possible. Add the pectin-destroying enzyme and a Campden tablet, cover, and leave for 24 hours. Stir in the sugar until it has dissolved and add the yeast and yeast nutrient. Cover securely and ferment for four or five days, stirring daily.

Strain the liquid through a fine-mesh bag into a fermentation jar and fit a fermentation lock containing sterilizing solution. Put the jar in a warm place and allow to ferment to a finish so that the bubbling has stopped, the wine begins to clear, and the S.G. is close to 1·000.

Rack the clear wine into a clean fermentation jar, add a Campden tablet, and leave to mature for several months, racking again as necessary. Bottle the wine when it is perfectly clear. Mature for six to nine months.

Burnet wine

burnet flowers	2 quarts	2 l
sugar	2½ lb	1·1 kg
water	1 gallon	4·5 l
chopped raisins	1 lb	450 g
orange	1	1
lemons	2	2
yeast and yeast nutrient	1 sachet and 1 tsp	1 sachet and 1 tsp
tannin	1 tsp	1 tsp
Campden tablets		

Put the flowers into a fermentation bin, pour on the water, and add a Campden tablet. Cover and leave to soak for seven days, stirring daily.

Strain the liquid on to the sugar and raisins in another vessel. Add the juice and grated rinds of the orange and lemons, tannin, yeast, and yeast nutrient. Stir well, then pour the must into a fermentation jar and fit a fermentation lock containing sterilizing solution. Put the jar in a warm place and allow to ferment out. When fermentation has finished, the bubbling will stop, the wine will begin to clear, and the S.G. will be near 1·000.

Rack the clear wine into a clean fermentation jar and add a Campden tablet. Rack the wine again as necessary, until it is perfectly clear and ready for bottling. Do not drink for six to nine months.

Cherry wine

cooking cherries	4½ lb	2 kg
sugar	2½ lb	1·1 kg
water	1 gallon	4·5 l
chopped raisins	½ lb	225 g
citric acid	1 tsp	1 tsp
pectin-destroying enzyme	1 tsp	1 tsp
yeast and yeast nutrient	1 sachet and 1 tsp	1 sachet and 1 tsp
tannin	1 tsp	1 tsp
Campden tablets		

Remove the stalks and wash the cherries. Put them into a fermentation bin and crush them. Then pour on the boiling water. Cover and leave to cool. Remove as many stones as possible and add the raisins, citric acid, pectin-destroying enzyme, and a Campden tablet. Cover and leave for 24 hours.

Then stir in the sugar until it dissolves and add the tannin, yeast, and yeast nutrient. Cover and leave to ferment for five days, stirring daily.

Strain the liquid through a fine-mesh bag into a fermentation jar and fit a fermentation lock containing sterilizing solution. Put the jar in a warm place to ferment until the wine stops bubbling, begins to clear, and the S.G. is close to 1·000.

When fermentation has finished, rack the clear wine into a clean fermentation jar, add a Campden tablet, and store for several months. Rack the wine at intervals if a sediment forms and bottle when the wine is absolutely clear, using dark bottles if you have made a red cherry wine. Leave for nine months to a year before drinking.

Damson wine

damsons	4½ lb	2 kg
sugar	2½ lb	1·1 kg
water	1 gallon	4·5 l
chopped raisins	½ lb	225 g
pectin-destroying enzyme	1 tsp	1 tsp
yeast and yeast nutrient	1 sachet and 1 tsp	1 sachet and 1 tsp
Campden tablets		

Wash the damsons and remove any stalks. Put them into a fermentation bin and crush them by hand. Remove as many stones as possible. Add the raisins, pour on 4 pints (2·25 l) of water, add the pectin-destroying enzyme and a Campden tablet, and stir well. Dissolve the sugar in 3 pints (1·8 l) of boiling water. Let it cool and when lukewarm add it to the pulp. Then put in the yeast and yeast nutrient, cover well and ferment for seven days, stirring daily.

Strain the liquid through a fine-mesh bag into a fermentation jar, top up with water and fit a fermentation lock containing sterilizing solution. Put the jar in a warm place for fermentation to continue. When all fermentation ceases, the wine will stop bubbling, begin to clear, and the S.G. will be close to 1·000.

Rack the wine into a clean fermentation jar and put in a Campden tablet. Store the wine until it is brilliantly clear before bottling in dark bottles. Leave it to mature for nine months to a year before drinking.

Golden rod wine

golden rod flowers	2 quarts	2 l
sugar	2½ lb	1·1 kg
water	1 gallon	4·5 l
orange	1	1
lemons	2	2
yeast and yeast nutrient	1 sachet and 1 tsp	1 sachet and 1 tsp
tannin	1 tsp	1 tsp
Campden tablets		

Put the bright golden flowers into a fermentation bin together with the grated rind of the orange and lemons. Boil the water and pour it over the flowers. Cover and leave to cool. Then add the orange and lemon juice and a Campden tablet. Cover and leave for three or four days, stirring daily.

Strain the liquid through a fine-mesh bag into another fermentation bin and stir in the sugar until it has dissolved. Add the yeast, yeast nutrient, and tannin, and cover well. Leave the mixture to ferment for four or five days and stir thoroughly daily.

Strain the must into a fermentation jar, fit a fermentation lock containing sterilizing solution and put the jar in a warm place for fermentation to continue until it stops bubbling, the wine begins to clear, and the S.G. is close to 1·000.

When the wine has finished fermenting, rack off the clear liquid into a clean fermentation jar and add a Campden tablet. Rack again, as necessary, until the wine is absolutely clear, and then bottle. It should be ready to drink after three months.

Marigold wine

marigold flowers	2 quarts	2 l
sugar	2½ lb	1·1 kg
water	1 gallon	4·5 l
lemons	2	2
yeast and yeast nutrient	1 sachet and 1 tsp	1 sachet and 1 tsp
tannin	1 tsp	1 tsp
Campden tablets		

Crush the marigold flowers and put them into a fermentation bin together with the grated rind of the lemon. Boil the water and pour it over the flowers. Cover and leave to cool. When lukewarm add the lemon juice and a Campden tablet. Cover again and leave for three or four days, stirring daily.

Strain the liquid through a fine-mesh bag into another fermentation bin and stir in the sugar until it dissolves. Add the yeast, yeast nutrient, and tannin, and cover well. Leave the mixture to ferment for four or five days and stir thoroughly daily.

Strain the must into a fermentation jar, fit a fermentation lock containing sterilizing solution, and put the jar in a warm place to ferment to a finish. The wine will stop bubbling, begin to clear, and the S.G. will be near 1·000.

As the wine clears, rack into a clean jar and add a Campden tablet. Rack the wine again, as required, until the wine is perfectly clear, and then bottle. Keep it for at least six months before drinking.

Marrow wine

ripe marrow	4½ lb	2 kg
brown sugar	3 lb	1·5 kg
water	1 gallon	4·5 l
root ginger	1 oz	25 g
oranges	2	2
lemons	2	2
pectin-destroying enzyme	1 tsp	1 tsp
yeast and yeast nutrient	1 sachet and 1 tsp	1 sachet and 1 tsp
tannin	1 tsp	1 tsp
Campden tablets		

Use the whole marrow including seeds. Cut it into small cubes. Put the marrow into a fermentation bin together with the grated rind of the oranges and lemons and root ginger. Boil the water and pour it over the ingredients. Cover and leave to cool. When lukewarm add the pectin-destroying enzyme, tannin, yeast, yeast nutrient, and juice of the oranges and lemons. Cover well and leave for four or five days, stirring daily.

Strain the liquid through a fine-mesh bag on to the sugar and stir well until it has dissolved. Pour the must into a fermentation jar, fit a fermentation lock containing sterilizing solution, and put it in a warm place to ferment to a finish. The wine will stop bubbling, begin to clear, and the S.G. will be near 1·000.

When fermentation has stopped and the wine clears, rack it into a clean fermentation jar and add a Campden tablet. Rack monthly until no sediment forms, then store for several months before bottling. Leave for six months before drinking.

Meadowsweet wine

meadowsweet flowers	1 gallon	4.5 l
sugar	2½ lb	1.1 kg
water	1 gallon	4.5 l
chopped raisins	1 lb	450 g
citric acid	2 tsp	2 tsp
yeast and yeast nutrient	1 sachet and 1 tsp	1 sachet and 1 tsp
tannin	1 tsp	1 tsp
Campden tablets		

Put the meadowsweet flowers into a fermentation bin and add the raisins and sugar. Boil the water and pour it on, stirring the mixture well. Cover and leave to cool before adding the acid, tannin, yeast, and yeast nutrient. Cover well and allow to ferment for seven days, stirring daily.

Strain through a fine-mesh bag into a fermentation jar and fit a fermentation lock containing sterilizing solution. Put the jar in a warm place to continue fermenting until the bubbling stops, the wine begins to clear, and the S.G. is near to 1·000.

When fermentation has finished, rack off the clear wine into a clean fermentation jar and add a Campden tablet. Store the wine for several months, racking at suitable intervals, and bottle when the wine is perfectly clear. Mature it for six to nine months before drinking.

Oak leaf wine

oak leaves	2 quarts	2 l
sugar	2½ lb	1.1 kg
water	1 gallon	4.5 l
lemons	2	2
yeast and yeast nutrient	1 sachet and 1 tsp	1 sachet and 1 tsp
tannin	1 tsp	1 tsp
Campden tablets		

Pour the water into a large boiling pan, and heat until it boils. Dissolve the sugar in the water, then pour it over the green oak leaves in a fermentation bin. Cover and leave for 24 hours.

Strain the liquid into another vessel. Stir in the juice of the lemons, tannin, yeast, and yeast nutrient, and pour the mixture into a fermentation jar. Fit a fermentation lock containing sterilizing solution and put the jar in a warm place to ferment to a finish. The wine will stop bubbling, begin to clear, and the S.G. will be close to 1·000.

Rack the clear wine into a clean fermentation jar and put in a Campden tablet. Rack again, at intervals, until the wine is perfectly clear and ready to be bottled. Store for nine months to a year before drinking.

Peach wine

peaches	3 lb	1·5 kg
sugar	2½ lb	1·5 kg
water	1 gallon	4·5 l
chopped raisins	½ lb	225 g
citric acid	2 tsp	2 tsp
pectin-destroying enzyme	1 tsp	1 tsp
yeast and yeast nutrient	1 sachet	1 sachet
	and 1 tsp	and 1 tsp
tannin	1 tsp	1 tsp
Campden tablets		

Cut the peaches in half and remove the stones. Put the pieces of peach into a fermentation bin and mash by hand. Add the raisins, pour on 4 pints (2·25 l) of water and put in a Campden tablet. Dissolve the sugar in 3 pints (1·7 l) of boiling water and when it has cooled add it to the pulp. Add the acid, tannin, yeast, yeast nutrient and some pectin-destroying enzyme. Cover securely and leave the must to ferment for seven days, stirring well daily.

Strain the liquid through a fine-mesh bag into a fermentation jar and top up with water. Fit a fermentation lock containing sterilizing solution and put the jar in a warm place to finish fermenting until it stops bubbling, begins to clear, and the S.G. is near 1·000.

When the must has finished fermenting and the wine clears, rack it into a clean fermentation jar and add a Campden tablet. Rack the wine at intervals, until no more sediment forms, then bottle when it is perfectly clear. Store it for six to nine months before drinking.

Plum wine

plums	4½ lb	2 kg
sugar	2½ lb	1·1 kg
water	1 gallon	4·5 l
chopped raisins	½ lb	225 g
pectin-destroying enzyme	1 tsp	1 tsp
yeast and yeast nutrient	1 sachet	1 sachet
	and 1 tsp	and 1 tsp
Campden tablets		

Remove the stalks, wash the plums, and put them into a fermentation bin. Crush them by hand and remove as many of the stones as possible. Add the raisins and pour on 4 pints (2·25 l) of water. Put in the pectin-destroying enzyme and a Campden tablet and stir well. Dissolve the sugar in 3 pints (1·8 l) of boiling water and leave to cool. When lukewarm pour it over the fruit, then put in the yeast and yeast nutrient. Cover securely and leave to ferment for seven days, stirring daily.

Strain the liquid through a fine-mesh bag into a fermentation jar, top up with water and fit a fermentation lock containing sterilizing solution. Put the jar in a warm place, and ferment to a finish so that the bubbling stops, the wine begins to clear, and the S.G. is close to 1·000.

When the wine clears, rack it into a clean fermentation jar and add a Campden tablet. Store the wine, racking as necessary, until it is perfectly clear and ready for bottling. Bottle red plum wine in dark bottles. Leave it for six to nine months before drinking.

Redcurrant wine

redcurrants	3 lb	1·5 kg
sugar	2½ lb	1·1 kg
water	1 gallon	4·5 l
pectin-destroying enzyme	1 tsp	1 tsp
yeast and yeast nutrient	1 sachet and 1 tsp	1 sachet and 1 tsp
tannin	1 tsp	1 tsp
Campden tablets		

Remove any stalks and leaves, wash the redcurrants and put them into a fermentation bin. Crush well by hand and pour on 4 pints (2·25 l) of water, stirring well. Dissolve the sugar in 3 pints (1·8 l) of boiling water and pour it over the pulp. When the liquid is cool add the pectin-destroying enzyme, yeast, yeast nutrient, and tannin. Cover well and leave to ferment for seven days, stirring daily.

Strain the liquid through a fine-mesh bag into a fermentation jar. Top up with water, fit a fermentation lock containing sterilizing solution and put the jar in a warm place to ferment to a finish. The wine will stop bubbling, start to clear, and the S.G. should be close to 1·000.

When fermentation has finished, rack the clear wine into a clean fermentation jar, add a Campden tablet, and store for several months. Rack again if a deposit forms and bottle when the wine is perfectly clear into dark bottles. Do not drink for six to nine months.

Rose petal wine

rose petals	2 quarts	2 l
sugar	2½ lb	1·1 kg
water	1 gallon	4·5 l
lemons	2	2
yeast and yeast nutrient	1 sachet and 1 tsp	1 sachet and 1 tsp
tannin	1 tsp	1 tsp
Campden tablets		

Put the rose petals into a fermentation bin together with the grated rinds of the lemons. Boil the water and pour it over them, mashing the petals well. Leave the mixture to cool and when lukewarm add the lemon juice and a Campden tablet. Cover and leave to soak for three or four days, stirring daily.

Strain off the liquid through a fine-mesh bag on to the sugar, tannin, yeast and yeast nutrient. Stir well, then pour the liquid into a fermentation jar. Fit a fermentation lock containing sterilizing solution and put it in a warm place to ferment out. The wine should stop bubbling, start to clear, and the gravity should be close to 1·000.

When fermentation ceases and the wine clears, rack into a clean fermentation jar and add a Campden tablet. Store the wine for several months, racking as necessary, and bottle into dark bottles when it is perfectly bright and clear. Leave it for six to nine months before drinking.

Vine prunings wine

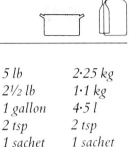

Vine leaves and shoots	5 lb	2·25 kg
sugar	2½ lb	1·1 kg
water	1 gallon	4·5 l
citric acid	2 tsp	2 tsp
yeast and yeast nutrient	1 sachet and 1 tsp	1 sachet and 1 tsp
tannin	1 tsp	1 tsp
Campden tablets		

Use the tender shoots and leaves pruned from a growing vine. Wash, then chop them up and put them in a boiling pan with the water. Bring to the boil, then simmer for half-an-hour. Leave to cool, then strain the liquid on to the sugar, citric acid, yeast, yeast nutrient, and tannin. Stir well before pouring the mixture into a fermentation jar. Fit a fermentation lock containing sterilizing solution and leave the jar in a warm place to ferment to a finish and until the bubbling stops, the wine starts to clear, and the gravity is close to 1·000.

When fermentation has ceased, rack the clear wine into a clean fermentation jar and add a Campden tablet. Store the wine for several months and rack again if a sediment forms. Bottle when the wine is absolutely clear. Leave it for six to nine months before drinking.

Whitecurrant wine

whitecurrants	3 lb	1·5 kg
sugar	2½ lb	1·1 kg
water	1 gallon	4·5 l
pectin-destroying enzyme	1 tsp	1 tsp
yeast and yeast nutrient	1 sachet and 1 tsp	1 sachet and 1 tsp
tannin	1 tsp	1 tsp
Campden tablets		

Remove any stalks, wash the whitecurrants, and put them into a fermentation bin. Mash them well by hand and pour on 4 pints (2·25 l) of water. Stir well and add a Campden tablet. Dissolve the sugar in 3 pints (1·8 l) of boiling water and pour this over the pulp. When the liquid is cool add the pectin-destroying enzyme, yeast, yeast nutrient, and tannin. Cover securely and leave to ferment for seven days, stirring daily.

Strain the liquid through a fine-mesh bag into a fermentation jar and top up with water. Fit a fermentation lock containing sterilizing solution and put the jar in a warm place to ferment out until the bubbling stops, the wine starts to clear, and the S.G. is close to 1·000.

When fermentation has finished, rack the clear wine into a clean fermentation jar, add a Campden tablet and store for several months. Rack again if a deposit forms and bottle when the wine is perfectly clear. Leave the wine for six to nine months before drinking.

Autumn recipes

Apple wine

apples	*4½ lb*	*2 kg*
sugar	*2½ lb*	*1·1 kg*
water	*1 gallon*	*4·5 l*
chopped raisins	*½ lb*	*225 g*
lemon	*1*	*1*
pectin-destroying enzyme	*1 tsp*	*1 tsp*
yeast and yeast nutrient	*1 sachet and 1 tsp*	*1 sachet and 1 tsp*
Campden tablets		

Chop the apples into small pieces and put them into a fermentation bin together with the raisins. Pour 4 pints (2·25 l) of cold water over the fruit. Dissolve the sugar in 3 pints (1·7 l) of boiling water, add this to the pulp, and leave to cool. When lukewarm, add the grated rind and juice of the lemon, the pectin-destroying enzyme, yeast, yeast nutrient, and a Campden tablet. Cover the bin securely and leave to ferment for eight or nine days, stirring and mashing the pulp daily.

Then strain the liquid off through a fine-mesh bag into a fermentation jar, top up with cold water, and fit a fermentation lock containing sterilizing solution. Put the jar in a warm place to continue fermenting until the bubbling stops, the wine starts to clear, and the S.G. falls to near 1·000.

When all signs of fermentation have ceased and the wine clears, rack it into a clean fermentation jar and add a Campden tablet. Store for several months, racking occasionally until the wine is perfectly clear and ready for bottling. Bottle and leave for six to nine months.

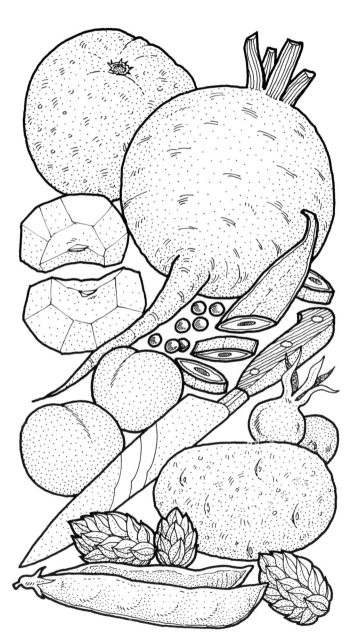

Beetroot wine

beetroot	4½ lb	2 kg
sugar	2½ lb	1·1 kg
water	1 gallon	4·5 l
chopped raisins	½ lb	225 g
citric acid	2 tsp	2 tsp
yeast and yeast nutrient	1 sachet and 1 tsp	1 sachet and 1 tsp
tannin	1 tsp	1 tsp
Campden tablets		

Scrub the beetroot, dice them, and put them into a pan with the water. Bring to the boil, then simmer gently for an hour. Strain the liquid on to the raisins and sugar in a fermentation bin. Stir until the sugar dissolves, then cover and leave to cool. When luke-warm add the acid, yeast, yeast nutrient, and tannin. Cover securely and leave to ferment for four or five days, stirring daily.

Strain the liquid through a fine-mesh bag into a fermentation jar. Fit a fermentation lock containing sterilizing solution and put the jar in a warm place to ferment out until the bubbling stops, the wine starts to clear, and the S.G. falls to 1·000.

When fermentation has finished, rack into a clean fermentation jar and add a Campden tablet. Rack again, as necessary, until the wine is absolutely clear and bright. Store for two or three months before bottling into dark bottles. Leave it for at least a year before drinking.

Blackberry wine

blackberries	4½ lb	2 kg
sugar	2½ lb	1·1 kg
water	1 gallon	4·5 l
chopped raisins	1 lb	450 g
pectin-destroying enzyme	1 tsp	1 tsp
yeast and yeast nutrient	1 sachet and 1 tsp	1 sachet and 1 tsp
Campden tablets		

Remove any stalks and pieces of leaf, wash the blackberries thoroughly, and put them into a fermentation bin. Mash the berries with a wooden spoon, then add the raisins. Pour the cold water over the fruit, stir well, and add some pectin-destroying enzyme and a Campden tablet. Cover the bin and leave the pulp for 24 hours. Stir in the sugar until it dissolves, then add the yeast and yeast nutrient. Cover securely and leave to ferment for five or six days, stirring and mashing the pulp each day. Strain off the liquid through a fine-mesh bag into a fermentation jar. Fit a fermentation lock containing sterilizing solution and put the jar in a warm place to ferment to a finish until the wine stops bubbling, begins to clear, and the S.G. is close to 1·000.

When fermentation has ceased, rack the clear wine into a clean fermentation jar and add a Campden tablet. Rack again as necessary, and store for several months before bottling into dark bottles. Leave it for nine months to a year before drinking.

Carrot wine

carrots	4½ lb	2 kg
sugar	2½ lb	1·1 kg
water	1 gallon	4·5 l
chopped raisins	1 lb	450 g
oranges	2	2
lemons	2	2
yeast and yeast nutrient	1 sachet and 1 tsp	1 sachet and 1 tsp
tannin	1 tsp	1 tsp
Campden tablets		

Scrub the carrots and put them into a boiling pan with the water. Bring to the boil, then simmer gently until the carrots are soft. Strain the liquid on to the sugar, raisins, and grated rind and juice of the oranges and lemons in a fermentation bin. Stir well and leave the mixture to cool. When lukewarm, add the tannin, yeast, and yeast nutrient. Cover and leave the must to ferment for five or six days, stirring daily.

Strain the liquid through a fine-mesh bag into a fermentation jar. Fit a fermentation lock containing sterilizing solution and put the jar in a warm place to ferment out. The wine should stop bubbling, start to clear, and the S.G. should be close to 1·000.

Rack the clear wine into a clean fermentation jar and add a Campden tablet. Store the wine for six months, racking when a sediment forms, and bottle when the wine is perfectly clear. Leave it for a year before drinking.

Celery wine

celery	4½ lb	2 kg
sugar	2½ lb	1·1 kg
water	1 gallon	4·5 l
chopped raisins	1 lb	450 g
citric acid	3 tsp	3 tsp
yeast and yeast nutrient	1 sachet and 1 tsp	1 sachet and 1 tsp
tannin	1 tsp	1 tsp
Campden tablets		

Wash the sticks of celery and cut them up into small pieces. Put them into the water in a boiling pan and boil for half-an-hour. Strain the liquid on to the sugar and raisins in a fermentation bin and stir well. Leave to cool then add the tannin, citric acid, yeast, and yeast nutrient. Cover securely and leave to ferment for five or six days stirring daily.

Strain the liquid through a fine-mesh bag into a fermentation jar. Insert a fermentation lock containing sterilizing solution and put the jar in a warm place to ferment to a finish. The wine should stop bubbling, start to clear, and the S.G. should be close to 1·000.

Rack the clear wine into a clean fermentation jar and add a Campden tablet. Rack again, as necessary, and store the wine until it is perfectly clear, before bottling. Leave it for six to nine months before drinking.

Elderberry wine

elderberries	3 lb	1·5 kg
sugar	2½ lb	1·1 kg
water	1 gallon	4·5 l
chopped raisins	½ lb	225 g
citric acid	2 tsp	2 tsp
yeast and yeast nutrient	1 sachet and 1 tsp	1 sachet and 1 tsp
Campden tablets		

Strip the elderberries from their stalks, wash them, and put them into a fermentation bin, together with the raisins. Boil the water and pour it over the fruit, mashing it well with a wooden spoon. Stir in the sugar until it dissolves, and leave to cool. Then add the acid, yeast, and yeast nutrient. Cover securely and leave to ferment for five days, stirring daily.

Strain the liquid through a fine-mesh bag into a fermentation jar. Fit a fermentation lock containing sterilizing solution and put the jar in a warm place to ferment until the bubbling stops, the wine starts to clear, and the S.G. is close to 1·000.

When fermentation has ceased, rack the clear wine into a clean fermentation jar and add a Campden tablet. Rack again, as required, until the wine is perfectly clear. Allow the wine to mature for several months before bottling into dark bottles. Leave it for at least eighteen months before drinking.

Grape wine

grape juice (not concentrate)	1 gallon	4·5 l
sugar	1½ lb	700 g
yeast	1 sachet	1 sachet
Campden tablets		

Extract the grape juice using a wine press and pour it into a fermentation bin. Stir in the sugar until it has completely dissolved and add a Campden tablet. Cover and leave for 24 hours. Then add the yeast and pour the liquid into a fermentation jar. Fit a fermentation lock containing sterilizing solution and put the jar in a warm place to ferment out until the bubbling stops, the wine starts to clear, and the S.G. is close to 1·000.

When fermentation has finished, and the wine clears, rack it into a clean jar and add a Campden tablet. Move the jar to a cool place and rack at monthly intervals. Bottle when the wine is absolutely clear and bright. Store the wine for at least six months before serving.

Greengage wine

greengages	4½ lb	2 kg
sugar	2½ lb	1·1 kg
water	1 gallon	4·5 l
chopped raisins	1 lb	450 g
citric acid	1 tsp	1 tsp
pectin-destroying enzyme	1 tsp	1 tsp
tannin	1 tsp	1 tsp
yeast and yeast nutrient	1 sachet and 1 tsp	1 sachet and 1 tsp
Campden tablets		

Wash the greengages, remove the stones, and put the fruit into a fermentation bin. Mash them well and add the raisins. Then boil the water and pour it over the fruit. Leave to cool, and when lukewarm add the pectin-destroying enzyme, acid, tannin, and a Campden tablet. Cover and leave for 24 hours.

Add the yeast and yeast nutrient, cover again and allow to ferment for four or five days, stirring and mashing the fruit daily.

Strain the liquid through a fine-mesh bag into a clean vessel and stir in the sugar until it dissolves. Pour the liquid into a fermentation jar, insert a fermentation lock containing sterilizing solution and put the jar in a warm place to ferment to a finish. The wine will stop bubbling, begin to clear, and the S.G. should be near 1·000.

Rack the clear wine into a clean fermentation jar, add a Campden tablet and store for several months. Rack at intervals, as a sediment forms, and bottle when the wine is perfectly clear. Leave for six to nine months before drinking.

Hawthorn berry wine

hawthorn berries	4½ lb	2 kg
sugar	2½ lb	1·1 kg
water	1 gallon	4·5 l
oranges	2	2
lemons	2	2
yeast and yeast nutrient	1 sachet and 1 tsp	1 sachet and 1 tsp
tannin	1 tsp	1 tsp
Campden tablets		

Wash the berries, put them into a fermentation bin, and pour on the cold water. Add a Campden tablet, cover, and leave to soak for a week, mashing the berries daily.

Strain the liquid through a fine-mesh bag into a clean vessel, and add the grated rind and juice of the oranges and lemons. Stir in the sugar until it dissolves, then add the tannin, yeast, and yeast nutrient. Cover and leave for 24 hours.

Then strain into a fermentation jar. Fit a fermentation lock containing sterilizing solution and put the jar in a warm place until fermentation has finished. The wine will stop bubbling, start to clear, and the S.G. should be near 1·000.

Rack the wine into a clean fermentation jar and add a Campden tablet. Rack again as necessary, then bottle into dark bottles when the wine is perfectly bright and clear. Leave for nine months to a year before drinking.

Hop wine

hops	3 oz	75 g
sugar	2½ lb	1·1 kg
water	1 gallon	4·5 l
chopped raisins	½ lb	225 g
bruised ginger	1 oz	25 g
citric acid	2 tsp	2 tsp
yeast and yeast nutrient	1 sachet and 1 tsp	1 sachet and 1 tsp
Campden tablets		

Put the hops and ginger into a pan with the water and bring to the boil. Then simmer for an hour. Strain the hot liquid on to the raisins and sugar in a fermentation bin. Stir until the sugar dissolves, cover, and leave for four or five days, stirring each day.

Then strain the liquid through a fine-mesh bag into a fermentation jar. Fit a fermentation lock containing sterilizing solution and put the jar in a warm place to ferment to a finish. The wine will stop bubbling, start to clear, and the S.G. will approach 1·000.

Rack the clear wine into a clean fermentation jar and add a Campden tablet. Rack again, if a further sediment forms, and bottle when the wine is perfectly clear. Leave for six to nine months before drinking.

Mulberry wine

mulberries	3 lb	1·5 kg
sugar	2½ lb	1·1 kg
water	1 gallon	4·5 l
chopped raisins	1 lb	450 g
pectin-destroying enzyme	1 tsp	1 tsp
yeast and yeast nutrient	1 sachet and 1 tsp	1 sachet and 1 tsp
tannin	1 tsp	1 tsp
Campden tablets		

Remove the stalks, wash the mulberries, and put them into a fermentation bin together with the raisins. Boil the water and pour it over the fruit, stirring well. Leave to cool, then add half the sugar, some pectin-destroying enzyme, tannin, yeast, yeast nutrient, and a Campden tablet. Cover securely and leave to ferment for four or five days.

Strain the liquid through a fine-mesh bag on to the remaining sugar in a clean vessel. Stir well, then pour the must into a fermentation jar and fit a fermentation lock containing sterilizing solution. Leave the jar in a warm place to ferment to a finish until the bubbling stops, the wine begins to clear, and the S.G. is close to 1·000.

When fermentation has ceased, rack the clear wine into a clean jar and store. Rack again as necessary until the wine is bright and clear and ready for bottling. Bottle into dark bottles and leave for nine months to a year before drinking.

Pea pod wine

pea pods	4½ lb	2 kg
sugar	2½ lb	1·1 kg
water	1 gallon	4·5 l
citric acid	2 tsp	2 tsp
yeast and yeast nutrient	1 sachet and 1 tsp	1 sachet and 1 tsp
tannin	1 tsp	1 tsp
Campden tablets		

Wash and cut up the pea pods. Put them into a pan with the water and boil for half-an-hour. Strain the liquid on to the sugar in a fermentation bin, and stir until it dissolves. Cover and leave to cool, then add the acid, tannin, yeast, and yeast nutrient. Pour the must into a fermentation jar, fit a fermentation lock containing sterilizing solution, and leave to ferment in a warm place. When fermented, the wine will stop bubbling, start to clear, and the S.G. will be close to 1·000.

When fermentation has finished, rack the clear wine into a clean jar and add a Campden tablet. Repeat the racking at monthly intervals until no more sediment forms. Then store the wine for several months before bottling. Leave it for six to nine months before drinking.

Pear wine

ripe pears	4½ lb	2 kg
sugar	2½ lb	1·1 kg
water	1 gallon	4·5 l
chopped raisins	1 lb	450 g
large lemons	2	2
yeast and yeast nutrient	1 sachet and 1 tsp	1 sachet and 1 tsp
Campden tablets		

Cut up the pears and put them into a boiling pan with the water. Bring to the boil, then simmer very gently for 20 minutes. Strain the liquid through a fine-mesh bag on to the sugar and raisins in a fermentation bin. Stir until the sugar dissolves, cover, and leave to cool. When lukewarm add the juice of the lemons, yeast, and yeast nutrient. Cover well and leave to ferment for four or five days, stirring daily.

Strain the liquid into a fermentation jar and fit a fermentation lock containing sterilizing solution. Put the jar in a warm place to ferment to completion until the bubbling stops, the wine starts to clear, and the S.G. is close to 1·000.

Rack the clear wine into a clean fermentation jar and add a Campden tablet. Rack again as necessary, and bottle when the wine is perfectly clear. Leave it for six to nine months before drinking.

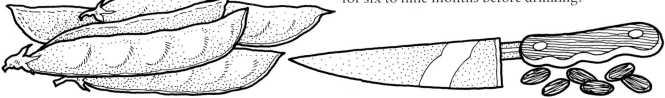

Potato wine

potatoes	4½ lb	2 kg
sugar	2½ lb	1·1 kg
water	1 gallon	4·5 l
chopped raisins	1 lb	450 g
oranges	2	2
lemons	2	2
yeast and yeast nutrient	1 sachet and 1 tsp	1 sachet and 1 tsp
tannin	1 tsp	1 tsp
Campden tablets		

Scrub the potatoes, cut them into quarters, and put them into a pan with the water. Bring to the boil, then simmer for 15 minutes. Strain the liquid on to the raisins and sugar in a fermentation bin, and stir well. Cover and leave to cool. When lukewarm add the grated rind and juice of the lemons and oranges, tannin, yeast, and yeast nutrient. Cover securely and leave to ferment for four or five days, stirring daily.

Strain the liquid through a fine-mesh bag into a fermentation jar, fit a fermentation lock containing sterilizing solution, and leave in a warm place to ferment out. The wine will stop bubbling, start to clear, and the S.G. should be close to 1·000.

When fermentation has finished, rack the clear wine into a clean fermentation jar and add a Campden tablet. Rack again, until the wine is absolutely clear, then allow to mature for two or three months before bottling. Leave it for at least nine months to a year before drinking.

Rosehip wine

fresh rosehips	4½ lb	2 kg
sugar	2½ lb	1·1 kg
water	1 gallon	4·5 l
chopped raisins	½ lb	225 g
citric acid	2 tsp	2 tsp
yeast and yeast nutrient	1 sachet and 1 tsp	1 sachet and 1 tsp
Campden tablets		

Wash the rosehips thoroughly and crush them. Put them into a fermentation bin with the raisins, acid, and sugar. Boil the water and pour it over the ingredients in the bin, stirring the pulp well. Cover and leave to cool. When lukewarm add the yeast and yeast nutrient, cover again, and allow to ferment for five or six days, mashing the pulp daily.

Then strain the liquid through a fine-mesh bag into a fermentation jar and fit a fermentation lock containing sterilizing solution. Put the jar in a warm place and leave to ferment to a finish. The bubbling will stop, the wine will begin to clear, and the S.G. will be close to 1·000.

Rack the clear wine into a clean fermentation jar and add a Campden tablet. Store the wine for several months, racking at monthly intervals, and bottle into dark bottles when perfectly clear and bright. Leave the wine for six to nine months before drinking.

Rowanberry wine

rowanberries	4½ lb	2 kg
sugar	2½ lb	1·1 kg
water	1 gallon	4·5 l
chopped raisins	1 lb	450 g
citric acid	2 tsp	2 tsp
yeast and yeast nutrient	1 sachet and 1 tsp	1 sachet and 1 tsp
tannin	1 tsp	1 tsp
Campden tablets		

Wash the berries and put them into a fermentation bin together with the raisins. Boil the water and pour it over the fruit. Cover and leave for three or four days, stirring daily. Then strain off the liquid on to the sugar in a clean fermentation vessel. Stir well, then add the acid, yeast, yeast nutrient, and tannin. Cover again and leave to ferment for seven days, stirring thoroughly each day.

Strain the liquid through a fine-mesh bag into a clean fermentation jar and fit a fermentation lock containing sterilizing solution. Put the jar in a warm place and allow to ferment out until the bubbling stops, the wine begins to clear, and the S.G. is close to 1·000.

Rack the clear wine into a clean fermentation jar and add a Campden tablet. Store the wine for several months, racking if a sediment forms, and bottle into dark bottles when it is perfectly clear. Leave it for nine months to a year before drinking.

Runner bean wine

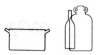

runner beans	3 lb	1·5 kg
sugar	2½ lb	1·1 kg
water	1 gallon	4·5 l
chopped raisins	½ lb	225 g
citric acid	2 tsp	2 tsp
pectin-destroying enzyme	1 tsp	1 tsp
yeast and yeast nutrient	1 sachet and 1 tsp	1 sachet and 1 tsp
tannin	1 tsp	1 tsp
Campden tablets		

Wash and slice the runner beans, then put them into a pan with the water. Bring to the boil, then gently simmer until they are soft. Strain the liquid on to the raisins and sugar in a fermentation bin, and stir until the sugar has dissolved. Cover and leave to cool before adding the acid, pectin-destroying enzyme, yeast, yeast nutrient, and tannin. Cover again and allow to ferment for seven days, stirring daily.

Then strain the liquid through a fine-mesh bag, into a fermentation jar. Fit a fermentation lock containing sterilizing solution and put the jar in a warm place to ferment to a finish. The wine will stop bubbling, start to clear, and the S.G. should be close to 1·000.

Rack the clear wine into a clean fermentation jar and add a Campden tablet. Repeat the racking at monthly intervals until the wine is perfectly clear. Store for several months to mature before bottling. Leave it for nine months before drinking.

Sloe wine

fresh sloes	4½ lb	2 kg
sugar	2½ lb	1·1 kg
water	1 gallon	4·5 l
chopped raisins	½ lb	225 g
yeast and yeast nutrient	1 sachet and 1 tsp	1 sachet and 1 tsp
Campden tablets		

Wash the sloes, put them into a fermentation bin, and crush them well by hand. Add the raisins and sugar, then boil the water and pour it on. Cover and leave to cool before adding the yeast and yeast nutrient. Cover again and leave to ferment for seven days, stirring daily.

Strain the liquid through a fine-mesh bag into a fermentation jar. Fit a fermentation lock containing sterilizing solution and put the jar in a warm place to ferment to a finish. The wine will stop bubbling, start to clear, and the S.G. will be close to 1·000.

When no further fermentation occurs, rack the clear wine into a clean fermentation jar and add a Campden tablet. Store for several months to mature, racking again if a sediment forms. Bottle the wine when it is perfectly clear and leave it for at least a year before drinking.

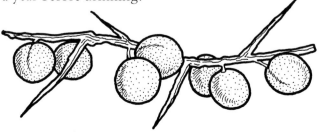

Sugar beet wine

sugar beet	4½ lb	2 kg
sugar	2½ lb	1·1 kg
water	1 gallon	4·5 l
chopped raisins	½ lb	225 g
bruised ginger	1 oz	25 g
citric acid	2 tsp	2 tsp
yeast and yeast nutrient	1 sachet and 1 tsp	1 sachet and 1 tsp
tannin	1 tsp	1 tsp
Campden tablets		

Scrub the sugar beet, cut them into chunks, and put them into a pan together with the ginger and water. Bring to the boil, then simmer for 30 minutes. Strain the hot liquid on to the sugar and raisins in a fermentation bin, cover, and leave to cool. When lukewarm stir in the acid, tannin, yeast, and yeast nutrient. Cover well and leave to ferment for four or five days, stirring daily.

Strain the liquid through a fine-mesh bag into a fermentation jar. Fit a fermentation lock containing sterilizing solution, put the jar in a warm place, and ferment to a finish. The wine will stop bubbling, start to clear, and the S.G. will be close to 1·000.

Rack the clear wine into a clean fermentation jar and add a Campden tablet. Store for several months, racking at intervals, until the wine is perfectly clear and ready for bottling. Leave it for nine months to a year before drinking.

Winter recipes

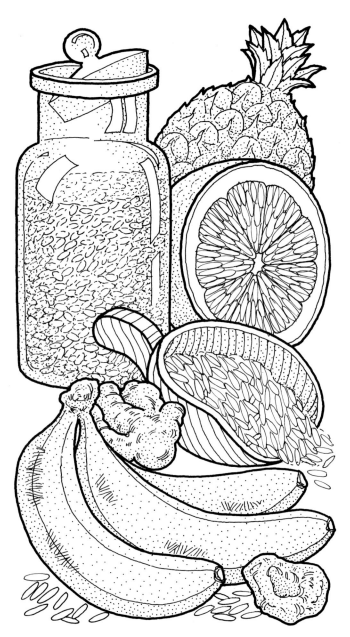

Apricot wine

dried apricots	2 lb	1 kg
sugar	2½ lb	1·1 kg
water	1 gallon	4·5 l
chopped raisins	½ lb	225 g
lemon	1	1
pectin-destroying enzyme	1 tsp	1 tsp
yeast and yeast nutrient	1 sachet and 1 tsp	1 sachet and 1 tsp
tannin	1 tsp	1 tsp
Campden tablets		

Put the apricots into a pan with the water and leave to soak for 24 hours. Bring to the boil, then simmer until the fruit is tender. Pour the hot mixture over the raisins and sugar in a fermentation bin, and stir thoroughly. Cover and leave to cool. When luke-warm add the grated rind and juice of the lemon, pectin-destroying enzyme, yeast, yeast nutrient, and tannin. Cover securely and leave to ferment for seven or eight days, mashing the pulp daily.

Then strain the liquid through a fine-mesh bag into a fermentation jar. Fit a fermentation lock containing sterilizing solution and put the jar in a warm place to ferment to a finish. The wine will stop bubbling, start to clear, and the S.G. will be close to 1·000.

Rack the clear wine into a clean fermentation jar and add a Campden tablet. Store for several months, racking as necessary, and bottle when the wine is perfectly clear and bright. Leave it for about six months before drinking.

Banana wine

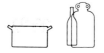

over-ripe bananas	4½ lb	2 kg
sugar	2½ lb	1·1 kg
water	1 gallon	4·5 l
chopped raisins	½ lb	225 g
large lemons	2	2
pectin-destroying enzyme	1 tsp	1 tsp
yeast and yeast nutrient	1 sachet and 1 tsp	1 sachet and 1 tsp
tannin	1 tsp	1 tsp
Campden tablets		

Put the bananas into a pan with the water and bring to the boil. Simmer gently for half-an-hour, then strain the hot liquid on to the sugar and raisins in a fermentation bin. Stir until the sugar has dissolved, cover, and leave to cool. When lukewarm, add the grated rind and juice of the lemons, pectin-destroying enzyme, yeast, yeast nutrient, and tannin. Cover securely and leave to ferment for six or seven days, stirring daily.

Strain the liquid through a fine-mesh bag into a fermentation jar and fit a fermentation lock containing sterilizing solution. Leave the jar in a warm place to ferment out. The wine will stop bubbling, start to clear, and the S.G. will be close to 1·000.

As the wine clears, rack it into a clean fermentation jar and add a Campden tablet. Store for several months, racking as further sediment forms, and bottle when the wine is completely clear. Keep the wine for six months or more before serving.

Barley wine

barley	1 lb	450 g
sugar	2½ lb	1·1 kg
water	1 gallon	4·5 l
chopped raisins	1 lb	450 g
scrubbed potatoes	1 lb	450 g
lemons	2	2
yeast and yeast nutrient	1 sachet and 1 tsp	1 sachet and 1 tsp
tannin	1 tsp	1 tsp
Campden tablets		

Put the barley into a fermentation bin together with the chopped potatoes, raisins, and sugar. Boil the water and pour it over the ingredients, stirring well. Cover and leave to cool. When lukewarm add the grated rind and juice of the lemons, yeast, yeast nutrient, and tannin. Cover again and leave to ferment for seven days, stirring daily.

Strain the liquid through a fine-mesh bag into a fermentation jar and fit a fermentation lock containing sterilizing solution. Put the jar in a warm place and allow to continue fermenting until the wine stops bubbling, begins to clear, and the S.G. is close to 1·000.

When fermentation has ceased, rack the wine into a clean fermentation jar and add a Campden tablet. Rack again at monthly intervals until the wine is perfectly clear, then bottle. Leave it for six months before drinking.

Date wine

dates	3½ lb	1·5 kg
sugar	2 lb	1 kg
water	1 gallon	4·5 l
citric acid	2 tsp	2 tsp
yeast and yeast nutrient	1 sachet and 1 tsp	1 sachet and 1 tsp
tannin	1 tsp	1 tsp
Campden tablets		

Chop the dates, remove as many stones as possible, and put the fruit into a fermentation bin with the sugar. Boil the water and pour it over the dates, stirring until the sugar has dissolved. Cover and leave to cool before adding the acid, yeast, yeast nutrient, and tannin. Cover again and allow to ferment for seven days, stirring each day.

Strain the liquid through a fine-mesh bag into a fermentation jar. Fit a fermentation lock containing sterilizing solution and place the jar in a warm place to ferment out. The wine will stop bubbling, begin to clear, and the S.G. will be close to 1·000.

When fermentation has finished and the wine clears, rack it into a clean fermentation jar and add a Campden tablet. Rack again if a sediment forms, and store for several months before bottling. Leave it for six to nine months before drinking.

Ginger wine

root ginger	4 oz	112 g
demerara sugar	3 lb	1·3 kg
water	1 gallon	4·5 l
chopped raisins	½ lb	225 g
lemons	4	4
yeast and yeast nutrient	1 sachet and 1 tsp	1 sachet and 1 tsp
tannin	1 tsp	1 tsp
Campden tablets		

Bruise the root ginger and put it in a pan with the raisins and sugar. Add the water, bring to the boil, then simmer for an hour. Pour the mixture into a fermentation bin, cover and leave to cool. Then add the grated rind and juice of the lemons, yeast, yeast nutrient, and tannin. Cover securely and allow to ferment for seven days, stirring daily.

Strain the liquid through a fine-mesh bag into a fermentation jar. Fit a fermentation lock containing sterilizing solution and put the jar in a warm place to ferment to a finish. The wine will stop bubbling, start to clear, and the S.G. will be close to 1·000.

Rack the clear wine into a clean fermentation jar and add a Campden tablet. Rack again, as necessary, until the wine is perfectly clear and ready for bottling. Store for several months before serving.

Grapefruit wine

large grapefruits	6	6
sugar	3½ lb	1·5 kg
water	1 gallon	4·5 l
chopped raisins	½ lb	225 g
pectin-destroying enzyme	1 tsp	1 tsp
yeast and yeast nutrient	1 sachet and 1 tsp	1 sachet and 1 tsp
tannin	1 tsp	1 tsp
Campden tablets		

Put the grapefruit peel and juice into a bowl together with the raisins and sugar. Boil the water and pour it over the ingredients, stirring until the sugar has dissolved. Cover and leave to cool before adding the pectin-destroying enzyme, yeast, yeast nutrient, and tannin. Cover again and allow to ferment for five or six days, stirring daily.

Strain the liquid through a fine-mesh bag into a fermentation jar. Fit a fermentation lock containing sterilizing solution and put the jar in a warm place to ferment to a finish. The wine will stop bubbling, start to clear, and the gravity will be near 1·000.

Rack the clear wine into a clean fermentation jar, add a Campden tablet, and store for several months. Rack again if a further sediment forms, and bottle the wine when it is completely clear. Leave it for six to nine months before drinking.

Lemon wine

large lemons	8	8
sugar	2½ lb	1·1 kg
water	1 gallon	4·5 l
chopped raisins	½ lb	225 g
yeast and yeast nutrient	1 sachet and 1 tsp	1 sachet and 1 tsp
tannin	1 tsp	1 tsp
Campden tablets		

Thinly peel the lemons, avoiding the white pith, and put them into a fermentation bin together with the lemon juice and raisins. Boil the water and pour it over the fruit. Stir in the sugar, until it dissolves, cover, and leave to cool. Then add the yeast, yeast nutrient, and tannin. Cover securely and leave to ferment for five or six days, stirring daily.

Strain the liquid through a fine-mesh bag into a fermentation jar. Fit a fermentation lock containing sterilizing solution and put the jar in a warm place to ferment to a finish. The wine will stop bubbling, start to clear, and the S.G. will be close to 1·000.

As the wine clears, rack it into a clean jar and add a Campden tablet. Rack again, as required, and bottle the wine when it is absolutely clear. Leave it for six to nine months before drinking.

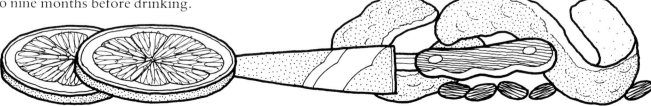

Maize wine

maize	2 lb	1 kg
demerara sugar	3½ lb	1·5 kg
water	1 gallon	4·5 l
chopped raisins	1 lb	450 g
large lemons	2	2
yeast and yeast nutrient	1 sachet and 1 tsp	1 sachet and 1 tsp
tannin	1 tsp	1 tsp
Campden tablets		

Soak the maize until it is soft, then drain it and place it in a fermentation bin. Add the raisins, grated rind and juice of the lemons, and sugar. Boil the water, pour it over the ingredients, and stir well until the sugar dissolves. Cover and leave to cool. When lukewarm add the yeast, yeast nutrient, and tannin. Cover again and leave to ferment for ten days, stirring the mixture daily.

Then strain the liquid through a fine-mesh bag into a fermentation jar. Fit a fermentation lock containing sterilizing solution and put the jar in a warm place to ferment to a finish. The wine will stop bubbling, start to clear, and the S.G. will be close to 1·000.

Rack the clear wine into a clean fermentation jar and add a Campden tablet. Rack again if a further sediment forms, and bottle the wine when it is perfectly clear. Store for several months before serving.

Melon wine

water melon	5½ lb	2·5 kg
sugar	2½ lb	1·1 kg
water	1 gallon	4·5 l
chopped raisins	½ lb	225 g
citric acid	2 tsp	2 tsp
pectin-destroying enzyme	1 tsp	1 tsp
yeast and yeast nutrient	1 sachet and 1 tsp	1 sachet and 1 tsp
tannin	1 tsp	1 tsp
Campden tablets		

Wash the melon, cut it into chunks, and put the pieces into a fermentation bin together with the raisins. Pour on the cold water, then stir in the pectin-destroying enzyme, acid, tannin, and a Campden tablet. Cover the mixture and leave it for 24 hours. Then add the sugar, yeast, and yeast nutrient. Cover again, and leave to ferment for five or six days, stirring each day.

Strain the liquid through a fine-mesh bag into a fermentation jar. Fit a fermentation lock containing sterilizing solution and put the jar in a warm place to ferment to a finish. The wine will stop bubbling, start to clear, and the S.G. will be close to 1·000.

When fermentation has ceased, rack the clear wine into a clean fermentation jar and add a Campden tablet. Rack again at monthly intervals until the wine is perfectly clear and ready to be bottled. Leave it for six to nine months before drinking.

Orange wine

large oranges	10	10
sugar	2½lb	1·1 kg
water	1 gallon	4·5 l
chopped raisins	1 lb	450 g
pectin-destroying enzyme	1 tsp	1 tsp
yeast and yeast nutrient	1 sachet and 1 tsp	1 sachet and 1 tsp
tannin	1 tsp	1 tsp
Campden tablets		

Grate the orange peel into a fermentation bin together with the raisins. Squeeze the orange juice into a jug and save it until later. Boil the water and pour it over the fruit. Stir in the sugar until it dissolves, then cover and allow to cool. Add the orange juice, pectin-destroying enzyme, yeast, yeast nutrient, and tannin. Cover securely and leave to ferment for five or six days, stirring daily.

Then strain the liquid through a fine-mesh bag into a fermentation jar. Fit a fermentation lock containing sterilizing solution and put the jar in a warm place to continue fermenting. The wine will eventually stop bubbling, start to clear, and the S.G. will be close to 1·000.

When all signs of fermentation have ceased, rack the wine into a clean fermentation jar and add a Campden tablet. Store for several months, racking occasionally, until the wine is perfectly clear and ready to be bottled. Leave it for six to nine months before drinking.

Parsnip wine

parsnips	4½ lb	2 kg
sugar	2½ lb	1·1 kg
water	1 gallon	4·5 l
chopped raisins	1 lb	450 g
citric acid	2 tsp	2 tsp
yeast and yeast nutrient	1 sachet and 1 tsp	1 sachet and 1 tsp
tannin	1 tsp	1 tsp
Campden tablets		

Scrub the parsnips, dice them, put them into a pan with the water, and bring to the boil. Simmer very gently until they are tender, then strain the liquid on to the raisins in a fermentation bin. Cover and leave to cool before stirring in the sugar. Add the acid, tannin, yeast, and yeast nutrient. Cover well and leave to ferment for four or five days, stirring daily.

Strain the liquid through a fine-mesh bag into a fermentation jar. Fit a fermentation lock containing sterilizing solution and put the jar in a warm place to continue fermenting. The wine will stop bubbling, start to clear, and the S.G. will be close to 1·000.

When fermentation has finished, and the wine clears, rack it into a clean jar and add a Campden tablet. Store for several months to mature the wine, racking if any further sediment forms, and bottle when the wine is clear. Leave it for at least a year before drinking.

Peach wine

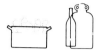

dried peaches	2 lb	1 kg
sugar	2½ lb	1·1 kg
water	1 gallon	4·5 l
chopped raisins	½ lb	225 g
citric acid	2 tsp	2 tsp
yeast and yeast nutrient	1 sachet and 1 tsp	1 sachet and 1 tsp
tannin	1 tsp	1 tsp
Campden tablets		

Soak the peaches in cold water for several hours until they are soft. Put them into a pan with the water, bring to the boil, then simmer for five minutes. Pour the hot mixture over the raisins and sugar in a fermentation bin, and stir thoroughly. Cover and leave to cool. When lukewarm add the acid, yeast, yeast nutrient, and tannin. Cover again and ferment on the pulp for five or six days, stirring and mashing the fruit daily.

Strain the liquid through a fine-mesh bag into a fermentation jar. Fit a fermentation lock containing sterilizing solution and put the jar in a warm place to ferment to a finish. The wine will stop bubbling, start to clear, and the S.G. will be close to 1·000.

As the wine clears, rack it into a clean fermentation jar and add a Campden tablet. Repeat the racking at monthly intervals until the wine is perfectly clear. Store for two or three months before bottling. Leave it for six to nine months before drinking.

Pineapple wine

pineapples	4	4
sugar	2½ lb	1·1 kg
water	1 gallon	4·5 l
lemons	2	2
yeast and yeast nutrient	1 sachet and 1 tsp	1 sachet and 1 tsp
tannin	1 tsp	1 tsp
Campden tablets		

Remove leaves and bottom stem and cut the pineapples into chunks. Put the pieces into a fermentation bin, boil the water and pour it over the fruit. Stir in the sugar, cover securely, and allow to cool. Then add the grated rind and juice of the lemons, yeast, yeast nutrient, and tannin. Cover securely and leave to ferment for five or six days, mashing the ingredients daily.

Strain the liquid through a fine-mesh bag into a fermentation jar. Fit a fermentation lock containing sterilizer and leave the must to ferment to a finish in a warm place. The wine will stop bubbling, start to clear, and the S.G. will be close to 1·000.

Rack the clear wine into a clean fermentation jar and add a Campden tablet. Rack again, as necessary, until the wine is perfectly clear before bottling. Leave it for about six months before drinking.

Prune wine

prunes	2 lb	1 kg
sugar	2½ lb	1·1 kg
water	1 gallon	4·5 l
chopped raisins	1 lb	450 g
citric acid	2 tsp	2 tsp
pectin-destroying enzyme	1 tsp	1 tsp
yeast and yeast nutrient	1 sachet and 1 tsp	1 sachet and 1 tsp
tannin	1 tsp	1 tsp
Campden tablets		

Put the prunes into a fermentation bin with the raisins. Boil the water and pour it over the fruit. Leave to cool. Add the acid, tannin, and pectin-destroying enzyme. Cover and leave for 24 hours. Then stir in the sugar, yeast, and yeast nutrient. Cover securely and leave to ferment for five or six days, stirring the mixture daily.

Strain the liquid through a fine-mesh bag into a fermentation jar. Fit a fermentation lock containing sterilizing solution, put the jar in a warm place, and leave to ferment out. The wine will stop bubbling, start to clear, and the S.G. will be close to 1·000.

When the wine clears, rack it into a clean fermentation jar and add a Campden tablet. Rack again at monthly intervals until the wine is absolutely clear, then bottle into dark bottles. Leave it for nine months to a year before drinking.

Raisin wine

chopped raisins	3½ lb	1·5 kg
demerara sugar	2 lb	1 kg
water	1 gallon	4·5 l
citric acid	2 tsp	2 tsp
yeast and yeast nutrient	1 sachet and 1 tsp	1 sachet and 1 tsp
tannin	1 tsp	1 tsp
Campden tablets		

Put the chopped raisins into a fermentation bin. Boil the water and pour it over the fruit. Cover and allow to cool before adding the acid, yeast, yeast nutrient, and tannin. Cover securely and leave to ferment for eight or nine days, stirring well daily.

Strain the liquid through a fine-mesh bag into a fermentation jar. Fit a fermentation lock containing sterilizing solution and put the jar in a warm place to finish fermenting. The wine will stop bubbling, start to clear, and the S.G. will be close to 1·000.

Rack the clear wine into a clean fermentation jar and add a Campden tablet. Repeat the racking as further deposits form, and store the wine for several months to mature. Bottle the wine when it is absolutely clear and bright, and store for six to nine months before serving.

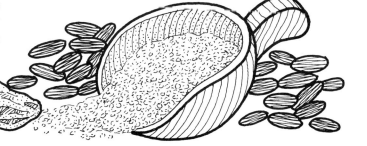

Rice wine

rice	3 lb	1·5 kg
sugar	2½ lb	1·1 kg
water	1 gallon	4·5 l
chopped raisins	½ lb	225 g
citric acid	2 tsp	2 tsp
yeast and yeast nutrient	1 sachet and 1 tsp	1 sachet and 1 tsp
tannin	1 tsp	1 tsp
Campden tablets		

Put the rice, raisins, and sugar into a fermentation bin. Boil the water and pour it over the ingredients, stirring well to dissolve the sugar. Cover and leave to cool, then add the acid, yeast, yeast nutrient, and tannin. Cover again and allow to ferment for seven or eight days, stirring daily.

Strain the liquid through a fine-mesh bag into a fermentation jar. Fit a fermentation lock containing sterilizing solution and put the jar in a warm place to ferment to a finish. The wine will stop bubbling, start to clear, and the S.G. will be close to 1·000.

As the wine clears, rack it into a clean fermentation jar and add a Campden tablet. Rack again, as necessary, until the wine is perfectly clear and bright, then bottle. Store for at least six months before serving.

Sultana wine

chopped sultanas	3½ lb	1·5 kg
demerara sugar	2 lb	1 kg
water	1 gallon	4·5 l
citric acid	2 tsp	2 tsp
yeast and yeast nutrient	1 sachet and 1 tsp	1 sachet and 1 tsp
tannin	1 tsp	1 tsp
Campden tablets		

Wash the sultanas and put them into a fermentation bin. Pour the water over them, then stir in the sugar, acid, yeast, yeast nutrient, tannin, and a Campden tablet. Cover securely and leave to ferment for five or six days, stirring thoroughly daily.

Then strain the liquid through a fine-mesh bag into a fermentation jar. Fit a fermentation lock containing sterilizing solution and put the jar in a warm place to continue fermenting. The wine will eventually stop bubbling, begin to clear, and the S. G. will be near 1·000.

When fermentation ceases and the wine clears, rack it into a clean jar and add a Campden tablet. Store for several months and rack again if further sediments form. Bottle when the wine is clear and bright, but store for at least six months before serving.

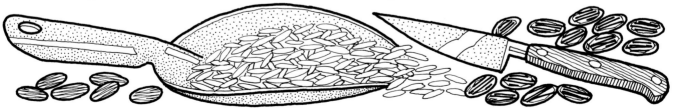

Tangerine wine

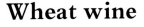

tangerines	12	12
sugar	2½ lb	1.1 kg
water	1 gallon	4·5 l
chopped raisins	1 lb	450 g
pectin-destroying enzyme	1 tsp	1 tsp
yeast and yeast nutrient	1 sachet and 1 tsp	1 sachet and 1 tsp
tannin	1 tsp	1 tsp
Campden tablets		

Squeeze the tangerine juice and save it for use later. Then grate the rinds into a fermentation bin. Add the raisins, boil the water, and pour it over the fruit. Stir in the sugar, making sure it dissolves, then cover and leave to cool. When lukewarm add the juice, pectin-destroying enzyme, yeast, yeast nutrient, and tannin. Cover securely, and leave to ferment for five or six days, stirring daily.

Strain the liquid through a fine-mesh bag into a fermentation jar. Fit a fermentation lock containing sterilizing solution and continue fermenting the must in a warm place. Eventually the wine will stop bubbling, start to clear, and the S.G. should be near 1·000.

When fermentation has finished and the wine clears, rack it into a clean jar and add a Campden tablet. Rack again at monthly intervals until the wine is absolutely clear. Bottle and store for several months before serving.

Wheat wine

wheat	1 lb	450 g
demerara sugar	3½ lb	1·5 kg
water	1 gallon	4·5 l
chopped raisins	1 lb	450 g
lemons	2	2
potatoes	2	2
yeast and yeast nutrient	1 sachet and 1 tsp	1 sachet and 1 tsp
tannin	1 tsp	1 tsp
Campden tablets		

Soak the wheat for several hours to soften the grains. Then put it into a fermentation bin together with the raisins, sugar, and sliced potatoes. Boil the water and pour it over the ingredients. Cover and leave to cool. When lukewarm stir in the juice of the lemons, yeast, yeast nutrient, and tannin. Cover well and leave for ten days, stirring the mixture daily.

Then strain the liquid through a fine-mesh bag into a fermentation jar. Fit a fermentation lock containing sterilizing solution and leave to ferment in a warm place until the wine stops bubbling, starts to clear, and the S.G. is near 1·000.

When fermentation has finished, rack the wine into a clean fermentation jar and put in a Campden tablet. Rack again as necessary until the wine is perfectly clear and ready to be bottled. Keep it for at least six months before drinking.

Serving wine

There is a great deal of snobbery and complicated ritual surrounding the serving and drinking of wine, most of which can be disregarded without spoiling your enjoyment. Some 'rules' are based on sound reasoning that certain wines are at their best when served chilled or in a particular type of glass, but common sense is of more use than any rule book. It is important, however, to ensure that the wine to be served is fully matured, free from any unpleasant flavours of yeast or *vinegar*, and is appropriate to the occasion for which it is being opened.

When choosing wine to serve with a meal it is worth remembering that it is usual practice to have white wine with fish, poultry, and white meats and red wine with red meat and game. Although it is not essential to follow this convention without question, it is often the case that a light dry wine will be most appreciated with fish or chicken, and a red fruity wine will accompany roast meat beautifully.

The only rule to follow is that of personal taste. The experience gained through a little thought and experiment is the best guide.

Temperature

Most red wine is at its best when served at room temperature, 60°F (15°C) to 65°F (18°C), although some red wines are very pleasant when served cooler than this.

White and rosé wines are usually best appreciated when they have been chilled for an hour or so in the refrigerator. Sparkling wines can be served quite cold, and this will help them to stay bubbly longer.

A temperature of about 45°F (8°C) will ensure that they do not go flat too quickly.

Glasses

The range of wine glasses available is extremely wide, with prices to suit all budgets. Personal choice will dictate the sort of glasses you buy, whether they are to be plain and simple or more decorative, or even extravagant.

All wine glasses should be thin and transparent, so that the colour of the wine can be clearly viewed and fully appreciated in all its hues. A tulip-shaped glass with a gently incurved rim will help to direct the *bouquet* upwards while containing it in the glass so that it may be enjoyed.

A glass with a stem is best, so that it can be held without touching the bowl. This ensures that a chilled wine is not warmed by hands grasping the bowl, and it also keeps the bowl free of fingerprints.

It is useful to serve sparkling wine in tall, thin glasses which look very elegant and also retain the bubbles for as long as possible.

Whatever sort of glasses are chosen, they should be filled between half and two-thirds full, not only because it is difficult to manoeuvre a glass filled to the brim, but more importantly so that there is enough space for the bouquet to collect and be savoured.

Opposite: Decanting a bottle of wine will ensure that any unwanted sediment is not poured into the glass.

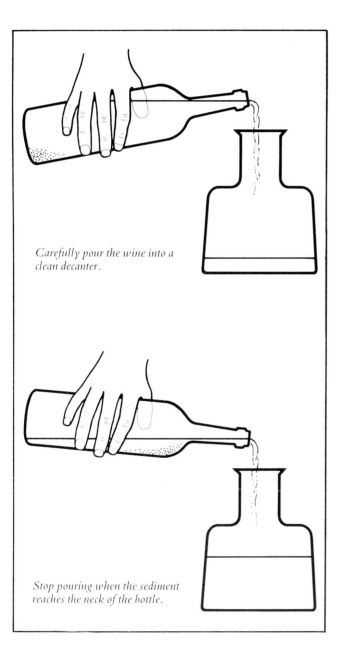

Carefully pour the wine into a clean decanter.

Stop pouring when the sediment reaches the neck of the bottle.

Decanters

Many wines benefit from being poured into decanters before serving, especially those wines which have thrown a sediment after they have been bottled.

To *decant* a bottle of wine, carefully pour it into a clean decanter, with a bright light behind the bottle so that you can see the sediment clearly. When the unwanted deposit reaches the neck of the bottle and is about to enter the decanter, stop pouring. With a little practice it is possible to ensure that only a small amount of wine is left in the bottle with the sediment, and these dregs need not be wasted as they can be used in the kitchen for adding to gravies and stews.

Wine looks most attractive when served from a decanter and, often, the process of decanting is beneficial to a wine because it allows any mustiness to be dispersed in the air, and the slight oxidation improves the wine's bouquet.

However you decide to serve your wine, remember that the care and patience required in all the previous stages of wine making is about to be tested, and a final effort will more than pay off.

What went wrong?

Sometimes, despite all your care, wine doesn't turn out as expected. It may even stop fermenting prematurely. Use this checklist to find and solve the problem.

Your wine smells and tastes of vinegar
There are probably only two things you can do: throw it away or wait until it turns completely into wine vinegar. The wine has been infected with the dreaded *vinegar fly*. You were probably not careful enough about sterilizing your utensils, or you may have left the wine exposed to the air for too long. Perhaps the water in the fermentation lock evaporated or you forgot to add any sterilizing solution to it. Be careful, though, that you have not mistaken vinegar for dryness—it would be a pity to throw away perfectly good but very dry wine which can easily be sweetened by the addition of a little sugar, or blended with another sweeter wine.

Your wine develops a haze which fining and filtering fail to clear
The haze is probably caused by starch if the wine has been made from root vegetables, or by pectin if you have made a fruit wine. You have forgotten to use a starch- or pectin-destroying enzyme or you have not used it in sufficient quantity. Keep the wine for your own use rather than serving it to friends: it should taste perfectly all right but it will have a less attractive appearance than bright wine.

You have made a red wine but it has become brown and cloudy
Sadly, you have allowed the light to get at it during fermentation or after it was bottled and it is prob-ably undrinkable. If you make sure that the acidity of the wine is correct, this will help to avoid browning but you should keep red wine out of the light at all times and it should always be stored in dark bottles and kept in a dark place.

Your wine develops whitish specks on the surface which eventually becomes oily
This is known as flowers of wine and is caused by a particular strain of wild yeast which converts the wine into carbon dioxide and water. If you allow it to remain, the wine will eventually become watery and lifeless. If you notice the effect when only a few specks of the yeast have developed you can treat it by adding two Campden tablets per gallon (4·5 l) of wine. Otherwise you should throw the wine away and be careful to sterilize all your utensils before using them again.

Your wine stops fermenting while it is still sweet, and the S.G. is much higher than 1·000
This is called a stuck fermentation and can be caused in a number of ways. It can usually be put right provided you make sure there are no other ailments such as 'off' odours.

You may have made your must too sweet so that the yeast is killed by the high concentration of sugar (check the recipe), or it may have reached its alcohol tolerance. You may be keeping the fermentation vessel in a place where the temperature is either too low or too high for the yeast to survive. The acidity may be incorrect. You may have used too many Campden tablets and these may have killed the yeast.

If the fermentation is stuck for any of these

Glossary

reasons, then you have not followed carefully enough the guidelines outlined in this book. But all is not lost. Give the wine a vigorous stirring with a clean wooden or polypropylene spoon. Check the acidity and temperature and note the S.G. Add some vitaminized yeast nutrient and this should get things going again. If after a few days, the wine is not bubbling vigorously again, make up a new starter bottle and add it to the wine.

Your wine smells and tastes strongly of sulphur dioxide
You have added too many Campden tablets. Eventually, it should disperse, but a vigorous stir will help.

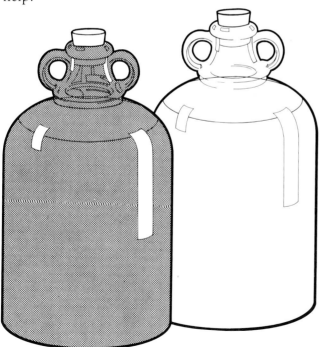

Acetification	the result of wine turning into vinegar after infection through the vinegar fly.
Aerobic	the first fermentation process that takes place when air is present.
Amylase	a substance that is used to prevent a starch haze from forming in the finished wine.
Anaerobic	the second fermentation that takes place in the absence of air which has been excluded by a fermentation lock.
Bentonite	a clay mineral that can be used in powdered form to clear wine.
Bouquet	the aroma of a wine.
Bung	a stopper made of cork or rubber which is used to close the neck of a fermentation jar. It may be pierced with a hole through which a fermentation lock can be inserted.
Campden tablet	sodium metabisulphite in tablet form for sterilizing wine or equipment when dissolved in water.
Capsule	a covering for the neck of a wine bottle after the cork has been inserted. It can be made of metal or a variety of plas-

tics and helps to exclude the air.

Decanting the method of pouring wine from its bottle into another container or decanter to allow it to breathe and to remove any debris from the wine.

Fermentation the process in which yeast feeds on sugars to produce carbon dioxide and alcohol.

Fermentation lock a device made of plastic or glass that allows gas to bubble out from the wine through water during fermentation and which prevents air from reaching the wine.

Finings any substance that can be mixed with wine to help it to clear.

Haze cloudiness that may occur in wine from, for example, the presence of starch or pectin.

Hydrometer a graduated instrument usually made of glass and weighted at the bottom to measure the specific gravity of wine or must.

Lees the sediment that forms and falls to the bottom of the wine during fermentation and maturing.

Maturation the improvement in the flavour of a wine that takes place when it is kept for months or even years. The alcohol content does not increase during this period.

Mead a wine made from honey.

Muselet a metal plate and wire cage that is used to hold a sparkling wine cork in place.

Must the sugary solution which is fermented with yeast to form wine.

Off-odours (tastes) smells (tastes) that suggest that something has gone awry.

O.G. the original specific gravity of the must before it has fermented.

Oxidation the exposure of wine to air causing it to discolour or even turn to vinegar.

Pectin a substance which is present in some ripe fruits and causes jam to set or may give a haze in wine.

Pectolytic enzyme a substance that is used to prevent a pectin haze from forming in the finished wine.

*p*H the acidity of the wine or

	must measured on a scale of 1 to 14.
Pitching	adding yeast to the wine.
Priming	adding sugar to a finished wine to cause a second fermentation in the bottle and give a sparkling wine.
Pulp fermentation	fermentation on the flesh, skin, and juice of a fruit or vegetable to extract the colour, flavour, and sugar.
Punt	the indentation in the bottom of some wine bottles in which any sediment that forms can settle.
Racking	siphoning clear wine from the lees.
Sodium metabisulphite	a chemical, often in powder or tablet form, which, when dissolved in water, can be used to sterilize wine and equipment.
Specific gravity (S.G.)	the weight of must or wine as compared with the weight of the same volume of water at a particular temperature.
Starter bottle	a small vessel containing a sugary solution together with acid and yeast nutrients in which yeast is allowed to begin a vigorous fermentation

	before it is added to the bulk of the must.
Vinegar	acetic acid which results from the oxidation of alcohol and which may be promoted by bacteria carried by the vinegar fly.
Vinegar fly	a fruit fly which carries acetifying bacteria.
Vinosity	the true body or wininess of a wine which only comes from the fermentation of the juice of the grape.
Yeast	an organism which is able to feed on sugary solutions to produce alcohol and carbon dioxide as by-products.
Yeast nutrient	mineral salts, vitamins, and other substances in small quantities which provide ideal conditions in which yeast can reproduce and produce alcohol.

Index

Page numbers in italic refer to illustrations.

Acid   15, 16, 19, 55, 66
    citric   13, 15, 17, 19, 25, 31, 55, 56, 60, 66, *67*
    lactic   15, 65
    malic   15, 65
    tartaric   15
Acidity   15, 16, 31, 114
    paper   *32*, 66, *67*
Alcohol   10, 11, 13, 16, 17, 19, 20, 23, 24, 35, 114
Ammonium sulphate   15
Amylase   40, 115
Apples   30, 40, 60
    juice   30
    wine   60, 92
Apricots   39
    wine   73, 102

Bacteria   9, 10, 29, 45, 53, 65, 66
Balm wine   74
Banana wine   103
Barley wine   103
Bean, broad wine   84
    runner wine   100
Beaujolais   53
Beet, sugar wine   101
Bentonite   38, 115
Berries   25, 30, 71
    hawthorn wine   96
Bilberry   53
Blackberry wine   93
Blackcurrant wine   83
Blending   50, 51
Blossom, hawthorn wine   78
    lime wine   79
Boiling   25
    pan   9, 25, *25*, *26*
Bordeaux   13, 53
Bottles   *42*, 43, *43*, 45, 51
    brush   43, *44*
    champagne   60, *63*
    punted   50, *50*
Bottling   43, 47, 50, 53, 56
Broad bean wine   84
Bullace wine   84
Bung, rubber   10, 35, 115
Burgundy   13, 53
Burnet wine   85

Campden tablets   9, 10, 29, *29*, 35, *35*, *37*, 51, 53, 56, 60, *61*, 65, 66, 67, 114, 115

Capsules   *48*, 115
Carbon dioxide   7, 13, 31, 53, 60, 65, 114
Carrot wine   94
Celery wine   94
Chablis   53
Cherry   53
    wine   85
Claret   53
Clearing   26, 35, 53, 56, 60, 66
Clover, mead   74
    wine   75
Coltsfoot wine   75
Concentrates   *52*, 53, 54, *54*, 55
Containers   9, 35
Contamination   9
Corking   43, *46*, 47, *47*
    tools   45, 46
Corks   10, 45, *45*, 46, *47*, 50, *64*
Cowslip wine   76
Currant wine   76

Damsons   39
    wine   86
Dandelion wine   77
Date wine   104
Decanting   113, *113*, 116
Deposits   10, *18*, 19, 35, 38, 43, 50, 51, *64*, 113
Drosophila melanogaster   9

Elderberry   53
    wine   95
Elderflower wine   77
Equipment   *8*, 9, *11*

Fermentation   7, 9, 10, 13, 15, *15*, 16, 17, 19, 20, 24, 29, 30, 35, 43, 51, 53, 55, 56, 60, 64, 71, 114, 116, 117
    aerobic   17, 19, 115
    anaerobic   19, 115
    bin   9, 17, *18*, 26, *26*, 27, 29, *32*, *33*, 55, 56, *57*, 60, *61*, 66, *67*
    jar   10, *11*, *18*, 19, *19*, 30, 31, *33*, 35, 38, 50, 51, 53, *54*, 56, *58*, 60, *62*, 66, *68*, 70, 115
    lock   7, 9, 10, 19, 31, *33*, 35, *37*, 51, 53, 55, 56, *58*, 60, *62*, *63*, 68, 114, 116
    melolactic   65
    secondary   64
    vessel   9, 26
Filter   40, 60, 114
    kit   *41*
    paper   40, *40*, *41*
Finings   38, *38*, 60, 114, 116
Flogger   46, *46*, 47